Contrast Community

Contrast Community

Practicing the Sermon on the Mount

JAMES L. BAILEY

WIPF & STOCK · Eugene, Oregon

CONTRAST COMMUNITY
Practicing the Sermon on the Mount

Wipf & Stock
An Imprint of Wipf and Stock Publishers
199 W. 8th Ave., Suite 3
Eugene, OR 97401

www.wipfandstock.com

ISBN 13: 978-1-62032-564-3

Manufactured in the U.S.A.

To Judy,
my life's companion,
who lives the faith!

"The reign of God is composed of people
who 'sell' their power, possessions, and prestige in such a manner
that they enable conditions of powerlessness, poverty, and depression
in others to be alleviated."

—Michael H. Crosby, *Spirituality of the Beatitudes,* 49

Contents

Foreword

FOR THE RENEWAL OF the church in our post-Christian era, no text is more vital than Jesus' Sermon on the Mount. Whenever the identity and mission of the church have been endangered at times of profound confusion and crisis, this sermon has emerged anew to provide orientation as a living Word from God. Consider the vision of St. Francis, appealing to Jesus' blessing upon the peacemakers and lessons from God's creation. Imagine the strength for resistance against the Nazi takeover of the church generated by Dietrich Bonhoeffer's commentary on the Sermon on the Mount, entitled *Discipleship*. Recall the power for nonviolent civil disobedience, grounded in love for the enemy, as it took shape in the Civil Rights Movement under the direction of Martin Luther King Jr. Join the hunger for social justice of the liberation theologians of Latin America and Palestine, who take the Beatitudes of Jesus as the promise of God's righteousness for the poor and oppressed. Wonder at the truth and reconciliation process advocated by Desmond Tutu in the overcoming of apartheid, grounded in Jesus' teaching that we are to embody the contrast community. Each of these Christian visionaries drew core inspiration from Jesus' Sermon on the Mount.

Self-help books and media pundits offer advice that would have us build our lives upon a foundation of sinking sand. The storms of life flood down upon us and their counsel is washed away. The Sermon on the Mount establishes a foundation for building life upon solid rock. The teachings of Jesus, epitomized in Matthew 5–7, are the font of wisdom needed by the church in our time of confusion and crisis for rediscovering and practicing truly life-giving relationships with others. While these teachings of Jesus were wrongly interpreted for generations as an unattainable utopia, proclaimed only to convict us of our sinfulness, the church urgently needs to re-appropriate the Sermon on the Mount as the path for living as Christian community. Excellent scholarship, beginning with Bonhoeffer and most recently articulated by authors like Hans Dieter Betz and Ulrich Luz, makes crystal clear that the Sermon on the Mount was offered as a serious proposal for the Christian way of life—nothing less and nothing more.

James L. Bailey has devoted his career to the vocation of serving as a teacher of the New Testament for the renewal of the church and the life of the world. This book epitomizes his own dedication both to the substance of the Christian faith taught by Jesus and to methods of engaging Scripture that allow it to breathe anew into us the Spirit of God. *Contrast Community: Practicing the Sermon on the Mount* harvests the fruits of contemporary scholarship on the sociological setting of Matthew's Gospel and the place within it of the Sermon on the Mount. Drawing upon the best of both New Testament research and recent theological appropriation of the Sermon on the Mount, the author communicates its significance in a fresh and vital way. The book stands on its own as a fascinating and compelling commentary on the substance of the text.

At the same time, Bailey is a master teacher, and in this book he provides a resource to make master teachers of others. The structure of the book moves in each chapter from immersion in the world of the text, to engaging the implications of the text for our time, to imaginative aids for groups to practice creative study of the Sermon on the Mount. Readers will profit from the book on each of these levels: elaboration of New Testament insights into the Sermon on the Mount, wisdom for appropriating the theological meaning of the text for Christian community in our times, and a practical resource for studying and teaching the Sermon on the Mount in congregational life. Those who will employ the book for group study are advised to begin with the Appendix, which is itself a jewel for those who would learn to teach the Bible with renewed vitality and transforming skill. The discussion questions at the end of each chapter render the book imminently practical and user-friendly for interactive Bible study in congregations.

Bailey has immersed himself so deeply in the study of the Sermon on the Mount that these pages reverberate with testimony to the truthfulness of its radical claims. Anyone who has come to know Jim and Judy Bailey will recognize this book serves for them not only as a message to others but a claim upon their own lives. One of the most challenging aspects to the paradigm shift in interpreting the Sermon on the Mount, as articulated in this book, is the assertion that this is an agenda not so much for individual Christians but for the entire Christian community. Jesus would have us together be the salt of the earth, the light on the hill, the contrast community leavening this world with the yeast of God's kingdom. Those who seek the kingdom of God must pass through the eye of the needle. The Sermon on the Mount is our needle. Have our lifestyles become so encumbered and our souls so flabby that even conventional church involvement has become a thing of the past? Or, are we on the edge of a new era—perhaps catalyzed by Christian communities of the South—when the church in our context reclaims its identity and mission as the contrast community Jesus taught us to be, practicing the Sermon on the Mount in risky discipleship?

Craig L. Nessan
Reformation Day 2012

Acknowledgments

I HAVE STUDIED AND maintained a special interest in the Sermon on the Mount for over thirty years. As a result, thank-yous are due to many people along the way—including all those classes and congregational groups that willingly engaged with me as we pondered the teachings of Jesus and their contemporary relevance. While still teaching at Concordia College in Moorhead, MN, in the 1980s, I participated in a workshop in northern California where I learned an interactive model using questions and exercises for engaging Gospel texts—a process Walter Wink adapted and described in his book *Transforming Bible Study*. I owe much to that group experience and Wink's book.

Over the years since then, I too have employed this interactive process in various forms to engage the Sermon on the Mount more holistically. During over twenty years of teaching at Wartburg Seminary in Dubuque, IA, I have frequently facilitated a course on the Sermon on the Mount, including the Lay Academy with faculty colleague Dan Olson, who brought to the experience his keen awareness of social psychology experiments that illuminate human foibles and proclivities addressed by Jesus' teaching. Teaching pastors in Papua New Guinea was particularly helpful since it allowed me a cross-cultural engagement with Jesus' teaching in the Sermon on the Mount.

Colleagues at the seminary—including Frank Benz, Ann Fritschel, Peter Kjeseth, David Lull, Ray Martin, May Persaud, Gwen Sayler, and Stan Saunders of the Biblical Division—have been encouraging in my teaching and supportive of my efforts to commit to writing what has been an oral, interactive process in classrooms and congregations. Craig Nessan read the manuscript and made numerous suggestions for enriching and emboldening it. I greatly appreciate his help and willingness to write the foreword. Over the years a number of student research assistants provided useful feedback on this project—especially James Erdman, Bonnie Flessen, Anita Mohr, Layne Nelson, and Jon Strasman.

I make special mention of Joanne Wright, a friend who served as Music Director at the Lutheran congregation in Dubuque where my wife and I are members. She provided invaluable assistance in selecting the hymns and songs for each session.

My family has supported me in the lengthy process of writing this book. I am grateful to my sister and brother-in-law, Nancy and Charles Townley, who made suggestions for chapter titles, and especially my wife Judy, who encouraged me and provided positive feedback and editorial assistance as I completed this project. The dedication indicates the joy and inspiration Judy gives to my life.

Finally, my thanks are extended to Christian Amondson and the editors at Wipf and Stock Publishers, who efficiently and graciously guided me in the final stages of readying my manuscript for publication.

In a real sense, this project, designed to facilitate communities' engagement with Jesus' teaching in the Sermon on the Mount, is itself a communal effort. To all involved, I express my deepest gratitude and hope that they will, as I have, discover their encounter with Jesus' teaching to be energizing and life-giving.

Abbreviations

BIBLICAL SOURCES

ABD   *The Anchor Bible Dictionary*

BDAG   *A Greek-English Lexicon of the New Testament and Other Early Christian Literature*

NRSV   *New Revised Standard Version*

HYMNALS

BC   *Borning Cry* by John Ylvisaker, vols. 1 & 2

ELW   *Evangelical Lutheran Worship*

GTG   *Glory to God*

HFTG   *Hymns for the Gospels*

LBW   *Lutheran Book of Worship*

STF   *Sing the Faith*

TFBF   *This Far by Faith*

TFWS   *The Faith We Sing*

TH1982 *The Hymnal 1982*

TNCH *The New Century Hymnal*

TPH   *The Presbyterian Hymnal*

TUMH *The United Methodist Hymnal*

W&P   *Worship & Praise*

W&R   *Worship & Rejoice*

W&S   *Worship & Song*

WOV   *With One Voice*

Introduction

THROUGHOUT THE HISTORY OF the church, Jesus' teaching in the Sermon on the Mount (Matt 5:1—7:29) has garnered special attention. Today an overabundance of articles and books about the Sermon on the Mount has been published. So it is reasonable to ask, "Why yet another book on the topic?" This book is distinctive in its combination of accessible biblical scholarship and various methods for group engagement with the significant passages in the Sermon on the Mount (hereafter, SM). It is written primarily for pastors, religious professionals, and lay leaders of the church to guide them and their group participants into a deep interaction with these extraordinary texts. It is useful for college and seminary classes that are experimenting with holistic methods for engaging biblical texts. The book will benefit pastors in preaching on passages in the SM.

The overall design of the book is straightforward. Chapter 1 describes the proven transformative power of the SM to influence and shape individuals and communities. It also discusses the SM's central role in the whole narrative of Matthew in providing content for the church-community's discipling mission among the world's people (Matt 28:16–20). In Matthew's day, the movement from *a community taught by Jesus* to *a teaching community in mission* appears to have been undertaken in the midst of considerable conflict, the crucible in which the earliest house churches were having their identity and mission formed and tested. The SM played a central role in this process, and it can play a similar role today.

Chapters 2 through 14, the bulk of the volume, offer a format to facilitate a group's engagement with the important texts in the SM, beginning with the Beatitudes in 5:3–12 and concluding with the mini-parable about *hearers and doers* in 7:24–27. Each chapter begins with the NRSV translation of the respective text and then is organized into four segments for engaging the biblical passage—*Getting into the Text, Knowing the Cultural Context, Engaging the Text Today,* and *Dwelling in the Text.*

GETTING INTO THE TEXT

Our study of any particular passage in the SM begins with hearing and interpreting the text as it now stands. We attempt to take seriously *what the text says, how it says it,* and *what it does not say* —so as to avoid, as much as possible, importing our own thoughts and times into the text before us. In the first section, we seek to attend to the precise wording, observing the way the text is structured and how it employs language in order to assess the intended rhetorical impact on its audience. Whenever fruitful, we also focus on the placement of the passage in the larger sequence of the SM. This often yields additional insight.

KNOWING THE CULTURAL CONTEXT

The texts were initially heard by first-century people living in an agrarian Roman world. Unknowingly, we can read back into a text the assumptions and experiences of our own world. In actuality, that environment was quite different from our twenty-first-century life and should seem very foreign to us. Failure to take seriously the alien character of the biblical world causes us to misread or misunderstand texts. It is, therefore, important to discover what we can about the world behind the text, particularly those features that will illuminate the cultural, social, political, and religious realities a given passage assumes or addresses.

In the Roman Empire, for example, the ruling elite and those aligned with them comprised at most 5 to 7 percent of the total population, with the vast majority of people living without influence, leisure, power, or wealth. There existed no middle class as we have known in America. Varying degrees of poverty stalked most of the population. Some would eke out their subsistence from artisan skills, trade, or farming. Most people in Palestine lived on the edge. If crops failed or taxes and prices increased, they faced immediate crisis. Poor health was widespread. Infant mortality was shockingly high, with up to half of those born not reaching the age of ten. Among the vast majority of the population, life expectancy was thirty to forty years. Urban life was crowded, filthy, smelly, and dangerous, with constant threats, such as infectious diseases, raging fires, and ethnic animosities. Rural life also was precarious, with most people worried about food shortages, crop failures, exorbitant taxes, loss of land, and breakup of families. Our great-great-grandparents who lived in farming communities or contemporary residents in parts of Africa and Asia would more readily understand that life.

All this does not yet mention the lack of the infrastructure we take for granted in our world—electricity, medical care, instant communication, and rapid travel. For each text, some information about that cultural context helps readers know more about first-century life.

ENGAGING THE TEXT TODAY

The *world in front of the text* is our world. This section deals with how we are to understand and appropriate the text today. Intentional investigation of the text itself—what it says and how it says it—and the first-century historical and cultural world should prepare us for a serious engagement with the passage. Openness to the text as sacred Scripture implies that it projects a world of meaning with authority and consequences for our lives. The words of Jesus in the SM offer an alternative vision that can free us from our self-created worlds that constrict and confine us, squeezing out real life. Careful consideration of these texts alters our way of thinking and behaving.

DWELLING IN THE TEXT

Integral to a full consideration of a particular passage will be a series of discussion questions, one or more application exercises, two or three quotations, three or more songs, and suggestions for prayer. I selected songs from a number of hymnals to facilitate use by participants from various denominations (see page xv for the list of abbreviations that includes the full titles of the hymnals). In addition, there is always an option for one or more group participants to memorize the text—that is, to learn the passage by heart. These activities are strategically designed to invite group participants into a holistic interaction with the text, using several senses and more than rationality alone. Allowing enough time for a variety of experiences to engage the words of Jesus is crucial for the transformative process.

It is recommended that those leading the groups read the Appendix as well as the chapters of the book. The Appendix explains more fully the elements included in the segment *Dwelling in the Text*. Those participating in the group should read chapter 1 and then the chapter dealing with each particular SM text to be considered by the group. Groups can work through all fourteen chapters as a way to consider the entire SM or could divide the study into two parts with eight and then six sessions: Chapter 1 and the texts in Matt 5 (chapters 2–8) followed by the texts in Matt 6–7 (chapters 9–14). Selected chapters could be used as a Lenten series (e.g., chapters 4–8 on the "antitheses" following an introductory session on the Beatitudes) or in a retreat weekend. Both adults and teenagers can benefit from working with these materials on the SM. Pastors could also utilize this book as a resource for developing a preaching series on the SM.

Leaders have additional responsibility to plan each session carefully by determining the time available and its best use. They need to decide how much, if any, of the first three sections in a chapter should be read and/or discussed, and which questions, exercises, quotes, songs, and prayers should be selected from *Dwelling in the Text* to facilitate the group's honest and full engagement with the text. The leader can choose to use most of the questions or, if group time is limited to less than an hour, only the starred questions. The leader could choose to utilize *lectio divina* as described in the Appendix, page 155, to foster a more meditative engagement with the passage. Strategic use of the process of mutual invitation can encourage everyone's participation (see the Appendix, page 156).

Finally, as author of this study it is important that I briefly describe myself. The particulars of my biography and social location shape my perspective and understanding. I am a white male, now over seventy years old, married, with two grown sons, who have their own families. After serving as pastor of a Lutheran congregation in Cincinnati, I have resided and taught the New Testament in Midwest America for most of my life (Ohio, Minnesota, and Iowa). Although I have often traveled outside the United States and Europe (e.g., Middle East, Africa, and Papua New Guinea) and although my wife and I have welcomed both a Kurdish and Vietnamese refugee to live with us in our home, I am primarily conditioned by Western culture and education. All my experiences and learning have enriched my engagement with the SM, but obviously who I am and where I have lived have also limited this engagement. That is why this book encourages the voices of others to join the consideration of these powerful texts.

May you join this conversation with others, and may your journey together through the SM be challenging, rewarding, and even transformative!

1

Power to Transform Communities

THE SERMON ON THE Mount (SM) in Matt 5:1—7:29 has long captivated me. For over thirty years, I have pondered these words of Jesus with their power to shape the perception and behavior of persons. These teachings can even transform communities into radically faithful followers of Jesus who live differently and have the courage to challenge injustices around them. During the early 1960s, I first read Dietrich Bonhoeffer's *Cost of Discipleship* and sensed the daunting challenge, yet deep joy, of following Jesus in the menacing Nazi years. Regarding his growing realization of the transformative power of the Bible, and especially the SM, Bonhoeffer testifies in a letter to a dramatic change in his own life that occurred sometime before 1933:

> Back then I was terribly alone and left to my own devices. It was quite awful. Then a change took place, a change that transformed my life and set its course in a new direction to this very day. I arrived at the Bible for the first time. Again, that is a terrible thing to admit. I had already preached quite often, I had seen much of the church, and both talked and written about it. But I had not yet become a Christian. In a wild and untamed way I was still my own master . . . In all my abandonment I was nevertheless quite pleased with myself. *It was the Bible which liberated me from this, especially the Sermon on the Mount.* Since then everything has changed. I could clearly feel it, and even other people around me noticed it. It was a great liberation. It

> became clear to me that the life of a servant of Jesus Christ has
> to belong to the church, and step by step it became ever more
> evident just how far this had to go ... The renewal of the church
> and the ministry became my supreme concern ...[1]

For Bonhoeffer, reading and engaging the SM were integral to his liberating experience that led him to see more clearly the radical nature of discipleship and the crucial importance of the church-community.

Faith communities and movements with significant social impact on the history of the last century, which were shaped by serious engagement of Jesus' teaching in the SM, include: Clarence Jordan and the Koinonia Farm, a racially integrated community in Georgia; Pastor André Trocmé and the Protestant town of Le Chambon in Southern France, who saved thousands of Jewish children and adults during the Nazi occupation; Brother Roger and the Taizé Ecumenical Community in France; and Dr. Martin Luther King Jr. and the civil rights movement in the 1960s.[2]

A more recent example occurred in East Germany. In 2007 and again in 2012, my wife and I visited St. Nicholas Church in Leipzig and learned of the indispensable role played by the SM in the weekly Prayer Services for Peace initiated by Pastor Christian Führer. These led to the huge, nonviolent street protests that toppled East Germany's Communist government and brought down the Wall. Horst Sindermann, a member of the Central Committee of the German Democratic Republic, said before his death: "We had planned everything. We were prepared for everything. But not for candles and prayers."[3] I would add—*the transformative power of the SM!*

HEARING AND DOING JESUS' TEACHING

Understanding the Sermon on the Mount involves *practicing* the SM. It is not enough to hear Jesus' words or even read and study them. We are *to do* them. In 7:24–27, Jesus declares that everyone who hears his words and *performs* them will be like a wise person who builds a house on rock.

---

1. Bonhoeffer, *Discipleship*, as quoted in the Editors' Afterword to the German Edition, 291. Italics are added for emphasis.

2. See Bonhoeffer, *Discipleship*; Jordan, *Sermon*; Hallie, *Lest Innocent Blood Be Shed*; and the writings of King.

3. Quoted in a pamphlet about St. Nicholas Church in Leipzig written by Pastor Christian Führer. For the story of what happened on October 9, 1989, see Jankowski, *Der Tag.*

The foolish person, in contrast, hears Jesus' words but *does not act on* them.

Teaching in antiquity was not done primarily for intellectual musing and reflection but as guidance for living. The words of prominent philosophers and teachers mapped out a way of living, wisdom for navigating the threats and unforeseen changes of daily existence. Only by creatively performing these teachings did a community of disciples begin to understand the words of their master. My son can instruct me a great deal about a computer program, but until I actually begin to operate the program I do not really comprehend what he has said. The teaching makes sense only as I am doing it. Likewise, a venerated conductor can interpret a richly-textured musical composition to members of his orchestra, but only when they perform their individual parts together under the maestro's expressive hands, do they begin to understand the symphony's magnificence and appreciate his interpretation. It is the *performance* of the conductor's interpretation of the musical notes that produces genuine *understanding*.

My purpose for this book is simple yet demanding—to present Jesus' teaching in the SM in ways that not only engage the interest and imagination of groups of people but also invite them into a deep dwelling in these extraordinary texts. As they do so, the group, no matter how small, will discover words of Jesus that sustain and stretch them, form and transform them as a community of ordinary people who seek to be life-giving Jesus-people in the places where they dwell. Again and again, Jesus' words create communities that make a divine difference in the world, striving to be *contrast communities* that embody an alternative vision and way of life within their host societies.

JESUS' TEACHING FOR COMMUNITY

The SM appears in the Gospel of Matthew. This Gospel was designed for house churches, probably in or near the city of Antioch in Syria sometime after the Romans' devastating destruction of Jerusalem and its temple in 70 CE. Its context is clearly late first-century Judaism in the Roman world.

The overall pattern of Matthew interconnects narrative and teaching sections. Despite different attempts at outlining Matthew, this much seems obvious—the Gospel includes five major blocks of Jesus' teaching:

1. Sermon on the Mount (5:1—7:29)

2. Mission Instructions (10:1—11:1a)

3. Parables of the Kingdom (13:1–53)

4. Community Instructions (18:1—19:1a)

5. Eschatological Teaching (24:1—26:1a)

The SM has prominence as the first teaching segment in the Gospel. It presents Jesus' foundational teaching for his followers, words intended to shape their sense of identity and mission. These words offer Jesus' vision of God's kingdom and how followers of Jesus are to live their life together.

When you track where the specific teachings of Jesus gathered in the SM appear in the other Gospels, you quickly discover two things. First, some sayings of Jesus appear only in Matthew's SM (e.g., *blessing the meek* in 5:5 and *pure of heart* in 5:8 or Jesus' words in 5:17–20); and second, other sayings exhibit a different form and/or occur in a quite different narrative context in the Gospel of Luke (e.g., the Lord's Prayer in Luke 11:2–4 or *Love your enemy* command in Luke 6:27–36). These discoveries suggest that the collection of Jesus' sayings in Matt 5:1—7:29 resulted from intentional compositional work. These particular words were gathered, ordered, and designed as the principal teaching of Jesus who speaks with divine authority. They are set on a mountain in Galilee, a place of revelation, and hence are called "The Sermon on the Mount."

One biblical scholar, Hans Dieter Betz, has argued that the SM corresponds to an *epitome* (a Greek word literally meaning "cut short" or "reduce") in the ancient Greco-Roman world.[4] *Epitome* designated a rhetorical, literary work that offered a condensation or summary of the important words of a significant teacher or philosopher. These core teachings of the master were meant to prompt followers to think and act flexibly in order to be faithful to their leader's vision and instruction in a variety of life situations. In Betz's own words, the SM as an *epitome* "is not law to be obeyed, but theology to be intellectually appropriated and internalized, in order then to be creatively developed and implemented in concrete situations of life."[5]

All this recommends that we who seek to follow Jesus Christ today take the SM seriously as his core instruction for our life together.

4. See Betz, *Essays*, 10–16.

5. Ibid., 16.

Communities, large and small, that have focused intentionally on these words of Jesus have been challenged and changed. This book is designed to facilitate such an open, sincere, and important engagement with the SM.

A TEACHING COMMUNITY OF JESUS' DISCIPLES

In the Gospel of Matthew, Jesus is the teacher *par excellence*. He is the teacher and master, and his followers are the disciples and servants (see 10:24–25). Matthew summarizes the Galilean activities of Jesus as *teaching, preaching, and healing* (4:23, 9:35). His disciples, in contrast, are instructed *to preach* the good news of the arrival of the reign of God and *heal* the sick, cast out demons, and even to raise the dead (10:7–8). Yet, they are not commanded *to teach*—at least during Jesus' earthly ministry.

The final scene in the Matthean narrative changes this. Matthew 28:16–20 pictures the eleven disciples on a mountain in Galilee meeting the risen Jesus, who instructs them to "make disciples of all peoples." They do so by *baptizing* and *teaching*. More precisely, the commissioning words of the risen Jesus direct them to "Go therefore and make disciples of all nations, baptizing them in the name of the Father and of the Son and of the Holy Spirit, and teaching them to obey everything I have commanded you" (28:19–20a). The main verb in verse 19, translated "make disciples," is only one word in Greek and implies drawing people into a close relationship with Jesus as his pupils,[6] as ones who are not only *informed* by his teaching but also *transformed* by it. To be drawn into the sphere of Jesus and his life-giving words is to become a community sharing his kingdom vision and *putting into practice his teaching*.

But how does this communal transformation take place? More often than not, 28:16–20 as the final scene in Matthew—what we call "the Great Commission"—has been treated and preached quite apart from any consideration of its role in the Gospel of Matthew as a whole. The commissioning words in verse 19 can be thoughtlessly detached from their narrative context and preached as Jesus' preeminent command to evangelize the entire world, with little or no attention to the pattern and purpose of the Gospel of Matthew.

---

6. *BDAG*, 609, expresses the basic meaning of *mathēteuein* as "to be a pupil, with the implication of being an adherent of the teacher."

If you view Matthew from the perspective of the church-communities for whom the narrative was written, the end of the story takes on new meaning. It could be argued that the end of story (28:16–20) is designed to direct the hearers' attention back to the beginning of the story—the opening chapters and especially the SM in 5:1—7:29. The *Great Commission* and the *Great Sermon* are linked both in the larger narrative of the Gospel and the experience of the followers of Jesus in the post-temple world of the first century. Both scenes take place on a Galilean mountain—a place of revelation and reverence (28:16 and 5:1). Both assume the authority of the risen Jesus (28:18 and 7:28–29) as "God with us" who accompanies and guides the church-communities in their life and mission (28:20 and 1:23). Both imply the community's identity is discovered precisely in undertaking mission (28:18–20 and 5:13–16). They are to engage in *missionary discipleship.*[7]

Thus, by design, the church-communities addressed by Matthew's Gospel are given an enormous mission that involves a movement outward from home base into the larger world. Their *discipling* efforts find concrete expression by *baptizing* others in the name of the Triune God and then by *teaching* them what Jesus has taught. The act of baptism draws the newcomers into the church, a worldwide community stretching far beyond any narrow and limiting group or sect. They are brought into this ground-breaking community that transcends all ethnic and social divides within the Roman world. They gain a new identity as members of the people of God.

Once incorporated within a local yet ecumenical Christian community, these newcomers are to be taught what Jesus shared with his earliest followers. Where do the church-communities addressed by Matthew find the teaching shared by Jesus? It is in the conveniently designed teaching blocks presented in the Gospel of Matthew. Thus, when the risen Jesus charges his communities to make others *his pupils by baptizing and teaching them*, the content of that teaching begins with the SM—his challenging words for molding and shaping the identity and vision of the community birthed by Jesus.

---

7. In his chapter "Matthew: Mission as Disciple-Making," *Transforming Mission,* 80, David Bosch states: "In attempting to articulate an identity for this community, Matthew draws on the tradition about Jesus of Nazareth. He clarifies the community's identity as an identity-in-mission by writing a gospel permeated, from beginning to end, by the notion of a mission to Jews and Gentiles . . . and by designing it in such a way that it would culminate in the 'Great Commission.'"

Leaders of these earliest Christian communities addressed by the Gospel of Matthew must have sensed the colossal challenge set before them—to teach and guide a disparate collection of people who by God's power had become a community of blessing for themselves and for others. If nothing else, the Matthean narrative is realistic about those who follow Jesus. They are *ones of little faith*, even those who would be leaders (6:30, 8:26, 14:31, 16:8, and 17:20). They trust the Lord Jesus and his message, it would seem, but under pressure they doubt and falter. The final scene in 28:16–20 accords with this portrait. The eleven disciples "see" the risen Jesus on a Galilean mountain and respond with both *worship and doubt*.

In spite of their *little faith*—or, better yet, because of it—the risen Jesus surrounds his commissioning words with a promise of his power and his presence. His post-resurrection communities of followers are given a world-encompassing mission already anticipated in the SM (see 5:13–16 with its "You are the salt of the earth" and "You are light of the world"). As resources for this mission the disciples are assured of the risen Jesus' presence (see again 28:20 and 1:23) and his power—the universal authority bestowed on Jesus because of his faithfulness to God's will to the point of his crucifixion (see 28:18 and 18:18–20). They are guaranteed his *powerful presence* for their life and mission as they share his teaching as epitomized in the SM. The challenge in their space and time is *to practice* the SM and *live like Jesus*, their teacher and risen Lord.

A JESUS COMMUNITY IN CONFLICT

The Gospel of Matthew, of which the SM is a crucial part, is the most Jewish of the Gospels. Its placement as first in the New Testament canon recognizes this. With its strong Jewish themes and recurrent references to Hebrew Scriptures, it functions as a bridge between the Jewish and Christian Scriptures. Matthew consistently characterizes Jesus as the Jewish Messianic figure whose person and activity fulfill the sacred texts (see, e.g., 1:1, 1:22–23, 2:5–6, 2:17–18, 4:14–16, 8:17, 12:17–21)—a claim confirmed for these earliest believers by witnesses to the resurrection of Jesus.

The Easter event separated Christian Jews from other Jews, since not all agreed to the claim about Jesus as Messiah. It is precisely in this field of contention that Matthew is encouraging his hearers to view the holy writings that testified to God's saving activities in former days through the prism of the Jesus-event. Hence, the Gospel of Matthew, in contrast to the synagogue-based Jews, places Jesus, not the Torah, at the interpretive center of Jewish history and life. It is Jesus who fulfills the Torah and the Prophets (5:17). It is Jesus, as the presence of God, who is greater than the temple (12:6). It is Jesus who is greater than Solomon (12:42). Jesus is heralded as the promised Davidic Messiah who comes to save his people from their sins (1:21) and to heal their diseases (8:17).[8]

Matthew's focus on Jesus, not the Torah, begins to explain the heightened tension in the narrative between Jesus and the scribes and Pharisees (see 23:1-36). In late first century, Matthew's communities and the Pharisee-led synagogues were competing for legitimacy as the rightful heirs of the Jewish heritage within the multifaceted Judaism of that day. The rabbinical movement, indebted to the Pharisees, would only later become the dominant form of Judaism. Charles Talbert points to the work of Gabriele Boccaccini in clarifying the new understanding of the relationship between Christianity and Judaism in the first century. He summarizes: "The blood tie between Christianity and Rabbinism [i.e., Rabbinic Judaism] is not to be conceived as parent (Rabbinism) and child (Christianity). The two are rather to be viewed as fraternal twins born of the same womb. Both are coherent developments of ancient Judaism."[9]

This awareness of the Matthean communities and their neighboring synagogues as sibling rivals within late first-century Judaism guides our approach to the SM. By utilizing the words of Jesus, Matthew is attempting to stake out the identity and mission of the Jesus-communities in the post-Easter and post-temple world in direct contrast to the Torah-obedient synagogues. He claims that these Christian communities are nothing less than God's called-out people, like Israel of old, whose communal identity reflects their mission to all peoples. As communities of Jews and Gentiles, they are part of God's embrace of all peoples. Divine mercy and justice had been embodied in the person and ministry of Jesus. Now they were called to exhibit that mercy and justice in their life together and world-embracing mission (28:18-20).

---

8. In the Gospel of Matthew, those in need of healing typically address Jesus as "Son of David" as they plea for mercy and help (see 9:27, 15:22, and 20:30-31).

9. Talbert, *Reading*, 4. For a fuller treatment of Matthew's relationship to the Judaism of his day, consult Talbert's chapter "The Setting of the Sermon: What is Matthew's Relation to Judaism?," 3-9.

Central to discovering their identity and mission is the practicing of the SM. As apprentices of Jesus, they are to practice what they are taught, to demonstrate in their daily existence coherence between their beliefs and deeds—or, in contemporary lingo, "to walk the talk." It is precisely the failure to practice what they teach that draws criticism from Jesus against his scribal and Pharisaic opponents in the Gospel narrative. His words to the crowds and his disciples, introducing the woes against the scribes and Pharisees, voice this scathing criticism of them: "The scribes and the Pharisees sit on Moses' seat; therefore, do whatever they teach you and follow it; but do not do as they do, for they do not practice what they teach" (23:2–3). As we will see, the SM also attacks this dichotomy between a person's creed and deeds (7:15–23) and insists on *putting into practice* the words of Jesus (7:24–27).

In this chapter, I have drawn attention to the rhetorical and transformative authority of the SM to influence and shape individuals and communities. The SM has made a difference in the history of the church and larger society, especially during the last century. I have also argued that the Gospel of Matthew, with the SM as the first of five teaching blocks, was originally designed to move the listening community of Christians from the point of just hearing the teaching of Jesus to putting his words into practice and to make it the centerpiece in church's discipling mission among all peoples throughout the Mediterranean world. The movement from a *taught community to a teaching community* was undertaken in the midst of conflict, the crucible in which the earliest Jewish Christian house churches had their Christian identity and vision of community and mission formed and tested. The SM was a central focus then and needs to play a similar role today.

2

Who Are the Blessed?—The Unlikely Ones

THE BEATITUDES (MATTHEW 5:3-12)

5:3 *Blessed are the poor in spirit,*

    for theirs is the kingdom of heaven.

5:4 *Blessed are those who mourn,*

    for they will be comforted.

5:5 *Blessed are the meek,*

    for they will inherit the earth.

5:6 *Blessed are those who hunger and thirst for righteousness,*

    for they will be filled.

5:7 *Blessed are the merciful,*

    for they will receive mercy.

5:8 *Blessed are the pure in heart,*

    for they will see God.

5:9 *Blessed are the peacemakers,*

    for they will be called children of God.

5:10 *Blessed are those who are persecuted for righteousness' sake,*

> *for theirs is the kingdom of heaven.*
>
> 5:11 *Blessed are you when people revile you and persecute you*
>
> > *and utter all kinds of evil against you falsely on my account.*
>
> 5:12 *Rejoice and be glad,*
>
> > *for your reward is great in heaven,*
> >
> > > *for in the same way they persecuted the prophets*
> > >
> > > > *who were before you.*

GETTING INTO THE TEXT

In Matthew, Jesus' Beatitudes were easily imprinted on the community's memory. The lead Greek word *makarioi* ("Blessed are . . .") is heard nine times. Members of the church-assemblies addressed by Matthew likely learned these words of Jesus by heart[1] and repeated these blessings as a reminder of the community's divinely bestowed identity and mission.

This pattern is different from Luke 6:20–26, where Jesus' four Beatitudes are matched by four woes.[2] Matthew includes only Beatitudes—two groups of four, each group culminating with a focus on righteousness or justice (5:6,10). While the first set of four emphasizes the community's pursuit of God's justice, the second set ends with the expectation of endurance in the face of opposition to God's ways. The first set describes the blessed recipients as *empty* and *lacking* what only God offers; the second set implies *fullness* supplied by God.[3] This carefully designed pattern of eight Beatitudes, spoken in the third person plural ("Blessed are *those* who . . ."), is followed by a ninth Beatitude that switches to the second person plural ("Blessed are *all of you* . . ."), hence directly reinforcing the

---

1. In Greek, the words describing the ones blessed provide an alliterative pattern, making memorization easier.

2. For example, "Blessed are you who are poor, for yours is the kingdom of God (Luke 6:20b) is matched by "But woe to you who are rich, for you have received your consolation" (Luke 6:24).

3. See Via, *Self-Deception and Wholeness*, 123–27. Via, 125, writes: "The first four are similar in that all of them express lack or emptiness. The lack of spiritual substance in the first is followed by the mourners, who lack joy, the meek, who lack power, and those who hunger and thirst for righteousness, and therefore obviously do not have it . . . The second four Beatitudes are similar because all of them express fullness. The merciful, the pure in heart, the peacemakers, and those who accept suffering for their righteousness are all morally or spiritually filled."

previous Beatitude regarding persecution. The concluding exhortation calls for an active response by the community—"*Rejoice and be glad,* for your reward is great in heaven, for in the same way they persecuted the prophets who were before you."

The same promise ("for theirs *is* the kingdom of heaven [God]") provides the rationale for the first and final blessing (5:3,10) and serves as a literary bracket for the series of eight. The participants in Jesus' community sense God's kingdom blessing *now* even in the midst of the Roman-ruled world (e.g., "Blessed *are* the poor in spirit" and "Blessed *are* the meek"). In addition, their hope-filled community focuses on *the future* that God will be enacting—e.g., "Blessed are those who mourn, for they *will be comforted*" with the passive voice implying they will be comforted *by God*. The community of Jesus still lives by faith, trusting that God's currently concealed ways *shall be disclosed* for all to see.

The 8 + 1 Beatitudes are designed for a community, not individuals. Their cumulative effect, when heard, puts a divine imprint on the community—how the community understands itself and views what God values and whom God honors. Jesus' Beatitudes point to the deep wisdom of how life works in the world God creates and reclaims. They shape how the community imagines and acts out the kingdom of God.

For a closer study of the Beatitudes in the Matthean sequence, read the "Notes on the Beatitudes" included at the end of this chapter. In doing so, sense the rich scriptural environment in which the Beatitudes resonate, as you note the numerous scriptural echoes made explicit.

KNOWING THE CULTURAL CONTEXT

The Beatitudes need to be understood in the context of Galilee where Jesus taught (27–30 CE) and in terms of audiences within the larger Roman world addressed by Matthew's Gospel in the last quarter of the first century.

As Jesus traveled in Galilee, he was announcing the reign of God largely to Jewish peasants whose traditional village economy was based on access to ancestral land for producing their food. Although there is little evidence that huge tracts of land in Galilee were controlled by the elites (Herodians, royal officers, and even wealthy priests), it is known that peasants were subject to pay taxes and tributes. Roman officials collected tribute to support their armies and government, a ruler like Herod

Antipas collected taxes for his building projects, and the priests expected tithes and offerings in support of themselves and the Jerusalem temple.

Given these multiple demands, up to one-third of a peasant family's crops could be taken, at times leaving the family with insufficient food resources for the year, particularly if there were poor crops or a drought. This intense pressure on peasants could lead to increasing indebtedness, with some losing their land and forcing them to become tenant farmers or even day-laborers, both of which are described in Jesus' parables (e.g., Mark 12:1–12 and Matt 20:1–15).

The opening Beatitude, especially as it is worded in Luke 6:20b, pronounces Jesus' blessing on those desperate ones who live on the edge: "Blessed are you who are poor, for yours is the kingdom of God." In Luke 6:24, this blessing is coupled with a warning to the wealthy who made demands on peasant families: "But woe to you who are rich, for you have received your consolation."

Matthew includes no woes but does employ the same Greek word (*ptōchoi*), which means the poor or destitute—those "economically disadvantaged," reduced to begging or dependent on others for support.[4] A different Greek word (*penēs*) describes a person "obliged to work for a living, but being reduced to begging"[5]—those today we label "the working poor." In Matt 5:3, the word is qualified with "in spirit," suggesting that Matthew's church-communities included more than the desperately poor. Nevertheless, these Christians were to sense their own poverty of spirit and to identify with the impoverished of society. God's blessing comes to those who find no hope in themselves or in the powers of this world.

ENGAGING THE TEXT TODAY

Familiarity with Jesus' Beatitudes can lead to our misunderstanding and domesticating these words. Jesus' initial blessing can be heard as undemanding comfort for the spiritually fatigued, where "poor in spirit" is understood as tired in spirit—or as even encouraging low self-esteem.

To first-century people immersed in a harsh world of poverty, violence, and death, the Beatitudes were unmistakably good news. For them, Jesus is speaking God's promises into their present uncertainties.

4. *BDAG*, 896.
5. Ibid., 795.

He pronounces God's blessing on the community of the poor in spirit, mourners, meek ones, those seeking justice, merciful ones, pure in heart, peacemakers, and those under attack because they act on behalf of Jesus' vision for God's world. These blessings describe a community *leaning into God's future.*

If many of us live in communities of faith not facing material deprivation or real threat, the Beatitudes in the SM could be seen as cheap grace. Yet, we too long for a blessing. We too can feel more cursed than blessed.[6] We too are insecure human beings searching for acceptance. Why is it that we in the U.S, one of the most affluent countries in the world, have such a high suicide rate? When asked, why do many disclose that they are not really happy and content with life?

Whether we fully realize it or not, we need relationships and our place in a community that rests under the blessing of God. Many Americans want therapy to help them cope, but they do not seek out community since community looms as a perceived threat to privatized lives.

There is an irony for those who prize individual freedoms and rights while desiring to limit their commitments to others. Only within the framework of community, where we risk relationships with others who could be a threat or nuisance, are our deepest human needs met. If we remain only in the crowd, avoiding community, we miss out on the shared life to which Jesus beckons us—serving others and living by a vision large enough to entertain the mystery of life. Jesus himself knew this and called people *out of the crowd into community*—one that is blessed precisely in its taking seriously his teaching about the kingdom of God.

A community residing under these divine blessings cannot help but seek ways to be a blessing to others, particularly the forgotten and forsaken of society. To quote Stanley Hauerwas and William Willimon, "if the preacher [Jesus] can first enable us to see whom God blesses, we shall be well on the road to blessedness ourselves."[7] We only become what we can envision.

In the blessed community, people discover together the deeply relational character of all life and the profound wisdom of each blessing. Individual Christians might not live into the fullness of each Beatitude, but together the community can reflect in amazing ways the blessings of God. A community can experience what it means to be more merciful

6. Nouwen's chapter entitled "Blessed" in *Life of the Beloved,* 67–83, is worth reading.

7. Hauerwas and Willimon, *Resident Aliens,* 84.

or more dedicated peacemakers because some members enact, at least partially, those Beatitudes. Together the community grows into the Beatitudes, reflecting the vision of God's preferred future, *a future Jesus speaks into the present.*

Jesus' vision reveals to us what and whom God blesses—those acknowledging their own spiritual poverty, those lamenting the gap between things as they are and as they ought to be, the gentle and non-cynical ones yearning and working for God's just ways, those who are merciful, those pure in heart desiring to know God, those who are making peace, and those who accept scorn and verbal abuse because they persist in doing righteousness.

Because its members take Jesus' Beatitudes so seriously, a Christian congregation stands in tension with its surrounding society. Such faith communities honor what and whom God honors, not what the popular culture demands. Striving for societal recognition can work against a faith community that welcomes all persons, including those judged by others as of little or no worth. A community shaped by Jesus' Beatitudes understands that all human beings are blessed by God and worthy of the community's honor and care.

DWELLING IN THE TEXT

Quotes:

- "I am increasingly aware of how much we fearful, anxious, insecure human beings are in need of a blessing. Children need to be blessed by their parents and parents by their children. We all need each other's blessings—masters and disciples, rabbis and students, bishops and priests, doctors and patients."[8]

- "The problem of modern living is that we are too busy—looking for affirmation in the wrong places—to notice that we are being blessed."[9]

- "I must tell you that claiming your own blessedness always leads to a deep desire to bless others. The characteristic of the blessed ones is that, wherever they go, they always speak words of blessing."[10]

8. Nouwen, *Life*, 68.

9. Ibid., 79.

10. Ibid., 82.

- "To give a blessing is to affirm, to say 'yes' to a person's Belovedness. And more than that: To give a blessing creates the reality of which it speaks."[11]

- "[T]he notion of human justice and compassion is rarely a foremost factor in ordering a community. Indeed, most communities find ways of treating it as the last question and never the first question about human reality."[12]

Questions:

Questions work best with groups of six to ten participants. For larger gatherings, divide into subgroups. If the session is less than an hour, you best begin with the starred questions. The leader may sometimes invite participants to discuss in pairs or use "mutual invitation" to encourage everyone's involvement (see Appendix, page 156).

*What content and patterns in the Beatitudes do you consider noteworthy? Why?

How do the Beatitudes empower oppressed people to live with hope?

*How do God's blessings compare to those blessings bestowed by our society?

Why might acting in accordance with Jesus' sayings provoke hostility from others?

*Describe a time when you felt reviled because you practiced your Christian faith?

What is it like to participate in a community blessed by God?

How have the experiences of suffering and joy gone together in your congregation?

*In what ways does your community of faith reflect the Beatitudes?

Which Beatitude(s) have you found expressed in your community or in your own life?

*Why are these words of Jesus both good news and a challenge for your congregation?

11. Ibid., 69.

12. Brueggemann, *Imagination,* 29.

Exercises:

1) Begin by posing the question: "How do God's blessings compare to those blessings bestowed by our society?" Instruct everyone in the group to write down two or three conventional beatitudes, examples of the types of individuals honored and blessed most often by our society and media. Encourage them to write these in a Beatitude form (e.g., *Blessed are the beautiful and youthful, for they can become anything they want* or *Blessed are the wealthy for they can enjoy the good life*), and then share these cultural blessings with the entire group as a way to highlight the striking counter-cultural character of Jesus' Beatitudes.

2) In pairs, have participants develop a deeper understanding of one or two Beatitudes by reading the notes at the end of the chapter on the assigned blessings and then create a way to enact them. After approximately fifteen minutes, invite the pairs to "act out" the Beatitudes in the proper sequence.

3) As a closing activity, invite the participants to form pairs and face each other. Instruct one partner to place his or her hand on the head or shoulder of the other person and repeat these words of blessings spoken in phrases by the study leader: (Name your partner) . . . *You are indeed loved by God . . . and gathered into a blessed community . . . to be a blessing to others . . . Live joyously . . . as a follower of Jesus.* Repeat the process so that the other partner also receives the blessing.

Songs:

"Blest Are They" (ELW, 728; GTG, 172; STF, 2155; TFWS, 2155; W&R, 666)

"Blessed Are the Poor in Spirit" (TNCH, 180)

"Be Not Afraid" (GTG, 243; W&R, 430)—especially verse 3

"The Beatitudes" (BC, 1:168)

"A Gift Will Come" (BC, 1:444)

"Rejoice in God's Saints," (ELW, 418; GTG, 732; TUMH, 708)

"Lead Me, Guide Me" (ELW, 768; GTG, 740; STF, 2214; TFWS, 2214)—especially for Matt 5:3

"Purify My Heart" (W&S, 3103)—focusing on Matt 5:8

"Prayer for a New Heart" (TUMH, 392)—spoken only, focusing on Matt. 5:8

Prayers:

O Blessed and Holy God, who has named Jesus the Beloved Son, continue to bless our community because of him and release that blessing through us to those around us. In Jesus' name. Amen.

Or you may wish to use the prayer circle to close your session (see Appendix, page 159).

NOTES ON THE BEATITUDES

Stanza 1

First Beatitude—Matt 5:3

In the first Beatitude, Jesus' blessing of the poor is qualified by "in spirit." If, as it seems likely, the phrase is here referring to "spirit" as the part of the human personality that is "the source and seat of insight, feeling, and will,"[1] then the scope of the blessing includes far more than the economically destitute. It includes any and all who are deeply conscious of their own impoverishment of spirit and are modest regarding their capacity to live righteously. They sense they must rely utterly on divine mercy and strength to live in God-pleasing ways.

Some scholars interpret the phrase "poor *in spirit*" as pointing to the powerless and exploited in the Roman world. Warren Carter writes, "Poverty not only physically damages people but also crushes people's spirits. It eats away at the very core of a person. Poverty deprives people of material resources as well [as] 'spiritual' ones such as hope, dignity, and value. These are the poor in spirit, those crushed by the empire into hopelessness and desperation."[2]

1. BDAG, 833.
2. Carter, "Power and Identities: The Contexts of Matthew's Sermon on the

"For theirs is the kingdom of heaven [God]" provides the reason for the blessedness of the "poor in spirit." The blessing of God's new reality is already present because of Jesus, something the spiritually impoverished realize. Through Jesus, they gain a vision of the way God values people and shapes relationships in community. This first Beatitude paves the way for all remaining blessings.

Second Beatitude—Matt 5:4

The Greek word (*penthountes*) in this blessing signifies an activity of mourning. In the ancient world, mourning was an important formalized process with prayers and rituals that included fasting, wearing sackcloth, and applying ashes (see Isa 58:5 and Dan 9:3).

What is unclear is the reason for mourning. Is the blessing on those who grieve over a death or their personal sins, or is it on those who sense the gap between things as they *are* in the world and things as they *ought to be*?

Likely serving as the scriptural background, Isa 61:1–3—utilized by Jesus in his hometown synagogue in Luke 4:18–19—answers this question. This Isaiah text connects the proclamation of good news *to the poor ones* with the announcement of comfort *to the ones who mourn in Zion*, offering hope to Jews living in Jerusalem after experiencing devastating defeat and exile at the hands of the Babylonians. For the Jews now back in Jerusalem, it is a time of confusion and hopelessness, when their daily life and circumstances do not match God's promises of restoration.

Third Beatitude—Matt 5:5

This beatitude has no parallel in Luke 6:20–26. It echoes a psalm that promises "But the meek shall inherit the land, and delight themselves in abundant prosperity" (Ps 37:11). As a whole, Ps 37 offers assurance to faithful people disheartened in the face of massive injustice and the apparent triumph of immoral and powerful people. The psalmist maintains that the wicked will not ultimately prosper; rather those who

Mount," 18, in Fleer and Bland, eds., *Preaching*.

are blessed by God will inherit the land. These "meek ones," as Ps 37:29 makes clear, are the "righteous ones."

Meekness accords with the content of the first Beatitude and names a way of thinking and acting that contrasts with the anger and brutality typical of those who disregard the will of God and the needs of other human beings. Meekness "is humility which is demonstrated in kindness."[3] Confronted with unchecked wickedness and injustice, the meek do not become bitter or rancorous, nor do they turn to violence. Rather they persist firmly and gently in the sure hope that God will rectify all things.

Gentleness as another synonym for meekness avoids the negative connotations often associated with the word "meek"—that is, a person viewed as timid, spineless, or unduly submissive. Meekness as gentleness implies a kind spirit joined to real strength. A saying posted on the office door of a former colleague, Ralph Smith, who was tragically killed in an auto accident on November 25, 1994, read: "Nothing is so strong as gentleness, nothing so gentle as real strength." During his ten years among us at Wartburg Seminary, Ralph exhibited this gentle strength.

In Matthew's Gospel, Jesus gives dignity to the word "meek." In 11:29 he declares, "Take my yoke upon you and learn from me; for I am gentle (same Greek word as *meek*) and humble in heart, and you will find rest for your souls." In 21:5—echoing Zech 9:9—Jesus' entrance into Jerusalem is described as that of a king "humble [*meek*] and mounted on a donkey . . ." Throughout Matthew, Jesus' life becomes the model of gentle strength for his community of followers—what is called for on their part to practice his teaching of nonviolent resistance to evil (5:38–42) and love of enemies (5:43–47).

Fourth Beatitude—Matt 5:6

In Luke 6:21a, the blessing rests on people with hunger pangs, whereas in Matthew this Beatitude completes the opening stanza and shifts the accent to those who "hunger and thirst" for *God's righteousness/justice*— for God's rectifying work on earth.

---

3. Luz, *Matthew*, 236.

The Greek word *dikaiosynē*, an important theme in Matthew, can be translated either "righteousness" or "justice." It first appears without explanation in the story of Jesus' baptism as Jesus replies to John's reluctance to baptize him: "Let it be so now; for it is proper for us in this way to fulfill *all righteousness*" (3:15). This same word occurs five times in the SM, suggesting that all righteous or just human action (5:10, 5:20, and 6:1 where it is rendered "piety" in NRSV) is bracketed and empowered by God's right ordering of things (5:6 and 6:33). *Dikaiosynē* is a relational term and represents the "moral ecology of the kingdom,"[4] where all things are working properly in right relationships.

Perhaps echoing Isa 49:10, the promise for this fourth Beatitude employs the strong metaphor of the blessed ones' having their hunger and thirst "satisfied by God." This alludes to the end-time banquet when all God's faithful people will sit together in the presence of God and Christ to experience the contentment only God can supply.

Stanza 2

Fifth Beatitude—Matt 5:7

The second group of four Beatitudes begins with a divine blessing on the merciful (see Luke 6:36). Mercy means identifying with the suffering of another person, resulting in action on behalf of that needy one. This Beatitude implies a close connection between human and divine mercy, a pattern elsewhere expressed in early Judaism: "He who is merciful to others, mercy is shown to him by Heaven, while he who is not merciful to others, mercy is not shown to him by Heaven."[5] Both the positive and negative side of this human-divine correspondence is later underscored by the petition on forgiveness in the Lord's Prayer (6:14–15) and in the parable of the unmerciful servant where the dire consequence of not passing on mercy is frighteningly dramatized (18:23–35).

In Matthew, mercy represents the essence of love and is far more important than the ritual of sacrifice (9:13 and 12:7; see also 23:23). By acting to put all things in right relationships, God acts mercifully

---

4. Leander Keck's phrase.

5. This saying is attributed to Rabbi Gamaliel Beribbi in the Babylonian Talmud, Shabbat 151b.

toward us, a gift we can pass on to others. Our being merciful is rooted in our repeated experience of God's mercy.

Sixth Beatitude—Matt 5:8

This Beatitude underscores a notion commonly accepted in Judaism. Worshippers are to have "clean hands and pure hearts," implying the inward sincerity and preparation needed in seeking communion with God (see Ps 24:4–6, Ps 51:10, Ps 73:1).

In biblical thought, "heart" is not narrowly understood as the seat of emotions. Rather it represents the center for feeling, thinking, and volition. Verse 8 thus entertains a comprehensive view of purity that gives central place to people's thinking and willing. Purity of heart entails far more than eliminating impure feelings and thoughts; it invites a focus of one's thoughts and will on the righteousness of God expressed in the kingdom activities.

The second part of the Beatitude offers a reason for the blessedness ("for they will see God"). It promises an unmediated experience of the presence of God, that which is the fervent goal of their life.

Seventh Beatitude—Matt 5:9

This Beatitude about peacemaking also resonates with a theme emphasized in the Judaism of Jesus' time. The Greek word for "peacemakers" (*eirēnopoioi*) makes obvious that those blessed are the ones who *make* peace. It involves active efforts towards reconciling hostile parties; it is not simply avoiding trouble. In the SM, peacemaking is a direct consequence of living in God's righteousness. It is the needed labor of a community participating in God's action of setting relationships right, both within the church-community (5:21–26) and beyond it when encountering antagonism (5:38–42 and 5:43–47).

It is quite appropriate to substitute the phrase "children of God" for "sons of God" in the Beatitude's promise, understanding this familial term as a reference to those who represent divine concerns on earth precisely because they are members of God's family. Peacemaking is at the heart of God's labor of love for this world and thus the pre-eminent task of Jesus' disciples in the present time.

Eighth Beatitude—Matt 5:10

The final Beatitude in the series of eight blesses those who are persecuted "for righteousness' sake." This last phrase clarifies the reason for the persecution. The blessed ones are those who so passionately yearn and work for the justice of God's kingdom here on earth (5:6) that their just behavior gets them in trouble.

It is as though persecution is a logical outcome of Christians' participation in God's new reign on earth. The commonwealth of God does not come without struggle and resistance from those invested in the status quo. The promise of inclusion in the kingdom of God (repeated from 5:3) rewards that difficult struggle

Ninth Beatitude—Matt 5:10–12

This additional blessing, reinforcing the eighth Beatitude, directly addresses Matthew's audience in the second person plural: "Blessed are you when people revile you and persecute you . . ." What was framed more indirectly in 5:10 now in 5:11 suggests the actual plight of the church-communities in Matthew's day. Because they identify with Jesus and his kingdom work ("on my account"), they are verbally insulted and maligned.

In 5:12, the pattern of "blessed are . . ." is broken with an invitation to rejoice. The community is called upon to "rejoice and be glad" in the midst of persecution. Though it seems paradoxical for people suffering persecution to rejoice, the community of Christ does experience joy in spite of its suffering because its members sense their living bears witness to God's justice and world-mending ways. They are to realize that they stand in the long line of the Jewish prophets who spoke God's word and acted in accord with it in spite of outright opposition. The promise of reward guarantees that God does not forget those who have persisted in the way of justice.

3

Blessed Community
—Called to Be Salt and Light

MATTHEW 5:13-16

5:13 *You are the salt of earth;*

   but if salt has lost its taste, how can its saltiness be restored?

   It is no longer good for anything,

   but is thrown out and trampled under foot.

5:14 *You are the light of the world.*

   A city built on a hill cannot be hid.

5:15 *No one after lighting a lamp puts it under the bushel basket,*

   but on a lampstand, and it gives light to all in the house.

5:16 *In the same way, let your light shine before others*

   so that they may see your good works

   and give glory to your Father in heaven

GETTING INTO THE TEXT

The blessings conferred by Jesus on his community of followers in 5:3–12
do not stand alone. They need the images in 5:13–16, those of salt and

light, which provide an antidote to any tendency of a mistreated community to disengage from its unfriendly environment. History offers numerous examples of religious communities with apocalyptic visions of the future that retreated from society. In these verses, Jesus counters such a world-forsaking inclination.

Matthew 5:13 is a remarkable statement, especially when compared with similar texts in Luke 14:34–35 ("Salt is good; but if salt has lost its taste, how can its saltiness be restored? It is fit neither for the soil nor for the manure pile; they throw it away . . .") and Mark 9:49–50 ("For everyone will be salted with fire. Salt is good; but if salt has lost its saltiness, how can you season it? Have salt in yourselves, and be at peace with one another . . ."). In Matthew, Jesus declares to his followers "*You are* the salt of the earth," thereby creating a powerful image for their identity and mission as a community. The plural *you*, placed first in the Greek sentence for emphasis, addresses not isolated individuals but the community as a whole, while the present tense verb *are* implies saltiness is a quality bestowed as part of their communal identity. It is not that they *must become* salt; rather together they already *are* salt. It is God's gift to them.

Yet this *gift* implies a *calling*. Note that 5:13 states "[All of] you are the salt *of the earth*." Salt by itself is not all that useful. It is not edible in any significant quantity, and too much of it can kill vegetation or make a field barren. Rather, salt has to be mixed with something else in order for it to be useful. Only a small amount of salt is needed to season, preserve, or purify the whole. The metaphor also applies to a community. Its saltiness is to be mixed with its environment, a tiny group affecting the larger society.

A little salt can have enormous power as long as it keeps its saltiness. Verse 5:13 indeed warns the community that salt is useful precisely because it is salt. If somehow its saltiness is lost—for example, by absorbing impurities—it is only good to be thrown out as waste material for a path or road. Similarly the special character of the Christian community should not be lost if it is to fulfill its role as a penetrating, transforming agent for the larger society.

In parallel form, Jesus describes the community's identity and mission with another image, that of light (5:14). Because of its frequent use within the biblical tradition, the image of light would trigger many associations for Jesus' first-century hearers. Already in 4:14–16, the author of Matthew has quoted Isa 9:1–2 to connect Jesus' public appearance with the "great light" promised for people of the Galilean territory sitting in darkness (cf. also John 8:12). Now his community of disciples shares in this illuminating activity in a dark and troubled world.[1] As with the image of salt, so too this one bestows on the Jesus-community both its identity (*"You are the light . . ."*) and its mission (*". . . of the world"*). It is a worldwide mission.

Jesus' final exhortation in this opening segment of the SM advances the figure of light, moving it from what the community *is* (*"You are the light of the world"*) to what it *does*. "In the same way, let your light shine before others, so that they may see your *good works* and give glory to your Father in heaven." Just as a burning lamp in the ancient world, by its very being, could illuminate a dark room and provide light for all around, so too the disciple-community's bestowed identity is to issue in activities that bear witness to God. The Christian community's *identity leads to mission*. The good deeds of its members are visible to others, who are moved to honor and praise God. Theirs are *good works that really work* for the glory of God and the benefit of others.

In the Gospel of Matthew, there exists no hang-up about good works. This contrasts with some Christians who misunderstand the Reformation's *grace alone* teaching and disdain any talk of good works. In Matthew, Jesus, the faithful Jew, repeatedly draws attention to the essential correspondence between what people *say* and what they *do* (see 7:15–20, 12:33–37, 23:2–3). It is not only *confession* that matters but also *public practice*. Such good works are not done to garner praise from others but function as transparent windowpanes to the caring *heavenly Father*, who creates and sustains a community's life. These deeds are not focused on self but on God as the source of all goodness and mercy. Here the Christian community's *witness by living* takes center stage, as Ulrich Luz notes,

> Verse 16b states the goal of Christian conduct: the works of the Christians have a missionary function. Here the Matthean priority of the deed over the word becomes clear. Just as discipleship means fulfillment of the commands of Jesus, so in the proclamation the *life* of the Christians receives a—not to say

---

1. See Isa 42:6, which designates the people of the covenant as "a light to the nations." Betz, *Sermon*, 160, writes: "At the time of the New Testament this self-understanding of Jews to be 'the light of the world' seems to have played an important role. This is all the more remarkable because of the political fact that Judea was an occupied country at the time. But the self-understanding as 'the light of the world' does not make claims in the sense of political power; rather, it aspires to enlightenment of the world in a religious or cultural sense."

the—decisive place. In such a conception of "Christianity of deed" a special office of proclamation cannot push itself imperiously into the foreground; witness by living remains the task of the whole community.[2]

Because 5:16 behaves like a summary to the previous verses, it is important to stress that the good deeds of Christians gain their content and shape from the Beatitudes in 5:3–12 and mission images in 5:13–15. Verses 13–16, taken as a whole, provide a significant conclusion to the Matthean Beatitudes that end by blessing a community under stress. Facing hostility, this community dares not withdraw from its host society but is sent forth as a blessed minority to share that blessing with the larger world—*blessed to be a blessing to others.*

KNOWING THE CULTURAL CONTEXT

It is helpful to recognize the importance of salt and light in the ancient world. Salt was an indispensable commodity, serving as a *preserving* (Ep Jer 1:28[3]—"Likewise their wives preserve some of the meat with salt, . . ."), *purifying* (2 Kgs 2:20–21—"[Elisha] said, 'Bring me a new bowl, and put salt in it.' Then he went to the spring of water and threw the salt into it, and said, 'Thus says the Lord, I have made this water wholesome; from now on neither death nor miscarriage shall come from it'"; see also Ezek 16:4), and *seasoning agent* (Job 6:6—"Can that which is tasteless be eaten without salt . . . ?"). Moreover, in the Jewish temple, salt was used in connection with grain offerings and other sacrifices (Lev 2:13, Ezek 43:24). This temple use has led some commentators to suggest that the salt metaphor in 5:13 intends to associate discipleship with life as *sacrificed* for the sake of the world. Salt evidently had a salutary effect on incense (Exod 30:34–35), and could also be used to sterilize fields (Deut 29:22–23, Judg 9:45, see also Jer 17:6). Finally, a phrase "covenant of salt," which appears in a number of passages (Lev 2:13, Num 18:19, 2 Chr 13:5), points to a meal with salt that forged a sacred bond between parties.[4] Analogous to

2. Luz, *Matthew*, 253. Italics are from the original text.

3. The Epistle of Jeremiah is an intertestamental writing, likely composed sometime before 100 BCE.

4. See Milgrom, *Leviticus 1–16*, 191–92, for his explanation of the covenant of salt. He writes: "Salt was the preservative par excellence in antiquity . . . A figurative extension of its preservative properties is the reference to the apostles as 'the salt of the earth' . . . in other words, teachers who guard the world against moral decay" (191). In the

salt's preservative function, Jesus' declaration asserts that his community of followers exercises a preservative role in society. Both Mark 9:50 and Col 4:6 may allude to this meal with salt, highlighting peacemaking (see 5:9) and gracious speech as essential to preserving society.

In the Greco-Roman world, salt was also associated with the worship of the gods. Because salt was so valuable as a preservative, it was distributed to Roman soldiers as part of their wages. We get the word "salary" from the Latin word for the phrase "to give salt." This practice lies behind the saying: "You're not worth your salt"—a huge insult in the ancient world.

In the biblical world, clearly salt was critical for well-being. The Jewish author Ben Sirach includes it in a list of necessities: "The basic necessities of human life are water and fire and iron and *salt* and wheat flour and milk and honey, the blood of the grape and oil and clothing" (Sir 39:26). It seems likely that Jesus' declaration to the Matthean community in 5:13 would resonate with multiple overtones for the hearers. Saying "You are the salt of the earth" is to assert that Christian community has a function in the larger world that is not only helpful and supportive but is indispensable to the health and life of the larger society.

Being "the light for the world" is equally critical. In a biblical environment without electricity, the importance of oil lamps and torches to illumine the darkness after sundown cannot be overestimated. To be in a pitch-dark setting without any illumination is both disorienting and frightening. In 5:14b, Jesus is possibly echoing Isa 2:2 by stressing that a city situated on a hill cannot be hid and thus functions to orient the traveler. Jesus further observes in 5:15, a lighted lamp within a house should not be covered, or it would not fulfill its intended function to dispel darkness. Light is to illuminate. Analogously, the community of Christ, in the way it lives and relates to its environment, is to present a visible alternative to the larger society. It exercises a universal function to provide light so all can see in a new way.

---

sixth century, Cyril of Palestine, recalling the final words of Euthymius, a monk of the Judean desert, includes this line: "Just as it is not possible to eat bread without salt, so it is impossible to practice virtue without love," quoted in Wilken, *Land*, 162.

ENGAGING THE TEXT TODAY

In North America today, businesses and groups publish mission statements.[5] Without a sense of mission and clarity about it, associations of people tend to lose their way or even disintegrate. Mission gives a community of people direction, purpose, and energy. Jesus' declarations and exhortation in 5:13–16 invite the disciple-community to recognize how inseparable are identity and mission. Some have emphasized that the church *does not have a mission*, but rather *it is mission*. Today's more common reformulation is: *The church does not have a mission. God's mission has a church.*[6]

Mike Lee, a Lutheran pastor in Wisconsin, uses the example of his family's dogs to illustrate the indispensable link between *identity* and *mission*. Their Australian Shepherds are intelligent dogs with strong herding and guardian instincts. Mike describes how easily these dogs become bored or even destructive when they are not given responsibilities: "Both play and work are important to Australian Shepherds, and when either is lacking in their daily routine, they become mischievous and dour. The good news about our dogs is that their behavior can be realigned by re-engaging them in one of their jobs or what they consider play."[7] *What they are doing* has to correspond to *who they are* as dogs. Analogously, congregations easily descend into bickering, pettiness, and even destructive behaviors when they are not engaged in activities worthy of their God-given *identity* and *mission*.

---

5. Stephen Covey et al., *First Things*, 106–7 and 307–21, even urge individuals to create mission statements in order to focus their activity around an intentional vision. They realize, however, that we do not generate mission just as individuals; mission emerges precisely in concert with others.

6. Roxburgh and Romanuk, *Leader*, xv, state: "God is about a big purpose in and for the whole of creation. The church has been called into life to be both the means of this mission and a foretaste of where God is inviting all creation to go. Just as its Lord is a mission-shaped God, so the community of God's people exists, not for themselves but for the sake of the work. Mission is therefore not a program or project some people in the church do from time to time (as in 'mission trip,' 'mission budget,' and so on); the church's very nature is to be God's missionary people. We use the word *missional* to mark this big difference. Mission is not about a project or a budget, or a one-off event somewhere; it's not even about sending missionaries. A missional church is a community of God's people who live into the imagination that they are, by their very nature, God's missionary people living as a demonstration of what God plans to do in and for all of creation in Jesus Christ."

7. Quoted from an email dated January 21, 2012, from Pastor Mike Lee.

Studies have demonstrated that many activities, assumed to make people happy, do not in fact bring contentment (e.g., playing golf or sunning on a beach every day). Rather, individuals register satisfaction and positive feelings when they are absorbed in some task that demands their full attention and uses their gifts. By shifting from a focus on themselves to a commitment beyond themselves, people feel more fulfilled and energized to complete important tasks.

Our society's promotion of self-satisfaction can produce a joyless existence and even depression. A community or group can also become preoccupied with itself and entertain no sense of mission to the larger society around it. As an exhilarating answer to this malaise, Jesus' opening words in the SM offer a community a *blessed life together*. These words are clear about God's purposes in the world and recognize humans' continuing need for worship and meaningful participation in extending *God's blessing to others*. At a profound level, a Christian community comprehends that its life together provides a powerful witness to others of what God intends life to look like. Their grace-filled living, which can even bear hardship and hostility, is inextricably connected with its blessing and mission in the world.

DWELLING IN THE TEXT

Quotes:

- What would it mean for a community "to live in such a way that its life together would not make sense if God did not exist?"[8]

> To be salt is hopeless.
> There is nothing so unhandy, so unmanageable,
> and so inedible than salt on its own.
> You can't do anything with salt alone;
> in a time of famine, you cannot eat it;
> in a time of drought, you can't drink it;
> it only would make things worse.
> Salt alone is no good;
> it makes the field unfertile, it kills life,
> it preserves death, it is heavy and useless.

8. These words are an adaptation of words uttered by Cardinal Suhard about Dorothy Day's obedience to follow Christ after her conversion in 1927. See Ellsberg, *By Little and By Little*, xv.

It becomes useful only when it is used
as Jesus indicates in the text today,
mixed up with other things,
and he explains as well how we should be mixed up.
We are not salt; we are the salt of the *earth*;
we should be mixed up with the *earth,*
we should be mixed with the reality around us.[9]

Questions:

Use the starred questions for a session less than an hour.

*What is Jesus saying in 5:13–16? Is anything surprising?

How crucial were salt and light to life in the ancient world?

*Why are salt and light appropriate images to describe followers of Jesus then and now?

*How do you recognize Jesus' sayings as both *gift* and *call*?

Why are the Christian community's identity and mission necessarily linked?

How do Jesus' declarations "You are the salt of the earth" and "You are the light of the world" encourage your community to think in fresh ways about ministry and mission?

*How is your church-community already salt and light for the neighborhood? How are you salt and light for your neighbors?

Why is it significant that Jesus' sayings about salt and light are minority images (that is, a little affects the whole)?

Should a community of faith be wary of doing "good works?" Why or why not?

*How do the Beatitudes in 5:3–12 shape your communal "good works"?

Exercises:

1) Provide supplies and invite participants to draw a picture of their community as either "the salt of the earth" or "the light of the world." Schedule

9. Donders, *Jesus,* 61–62.

about five to seven minutes for this exercise, and then allow a few minutes for an explanation of the sketches.

2) As a closing exercise, mention the "covenant of salt" (Lev 2:13, Num 18:19, 2 Chr 13:5) described in the chapter as a ritualized sharing of bread with salt to seal or signify a bond of loyalty between God and humans or between human beings. After briefly explaining this biblical covenantal practice, pass a whole loaf of bread with a small bowl of salt around the circle of participants. Instruct everyone to break off a piece of bread, dip it into the salt, and then, after all have a piece, eat it together. This ritual can represent the congregation as a covenantal community of salt for the sake of the world.

3) Place a table with one or more candles in the middle of the group. Darken the room, allowing all to experience the darkness for a few minutes. Light one candle and ask the group to ponder and respond briefly to the question: *What does it imply for the Christian community to be the light of the world?* After a period of silence, light more candles and invite the participants to sing one of the following songs or say the opening verses in Evening Prayer or Vespers in *Evangelical Lutheran Worship*:

Jesus Christ is the light of the world,   *the light no darkness can overcome.*

Stay with us, Lord, for it is evening,   *and the day is almost over.*

Let your light scatter the darkness   *and illumine your church.*[10]

Songs:

"We Are Called" (ELW, 720; STF, 2172; TFWS, 2172)

"Bring Forth the Kingdom of God" (STF, 2190; TFWS, 2190; TNCH, 181; W&P, 22)[11]

"Renew Your Church" (TNCH, 311; W&R, 462)

10. *ELW,* 309. A larger portion of the Vespers service featuring the image of light could be sung or said. This worship service is included in a number of worship books (see "O Gracious Light" in *TH1982,* S 59–61).

11. This hymn written by Marty Haugen includes verse one on "salt" and verse two on "light."

"This Little Light of Mine" (ELW, 677; TFBF, 65; TNCH, 524, 525; TUMH, 585)

"Christ, Be Our Light" (ELW, 715)

"Go, Make Disciples" (ELW, 540)

"We Are Marching in the Light of God" (ELW, 866; GTG, 853; STF, 2235-b; TFWS, 2235-b; TNCH, 526)

"Shine, Jesus, Shine" (ELW, 671; GTG, 192; STF, 2173; TFBF, 64; TFWS, 2173; W&R, 319)

"Gather Us In" (ELW, 532; STF, 2236; TFWS, 2236; W&R, 649)—especially verse 1

"Let Your Light Shine" (BC, 2:549)

Prayers:

"Be our light in the darkness, O God, and in your great mercy defend us from all perils and dangers of this night; for the love of your only Son, our Savior Jesus Christ. Amen."[12]

Or you may choose to use the prayer circle to close your session (see Appendix, page 159).

---

12. *ELW*, 326, as one of the closing prayers of the Night Prayer or Compline service.

4

Blessed Community
—Freed from Nursing Anger

MATTHEW 5:21-26

5:21 *You have heard that it was said to those of ancient times,*

    "You shall not murder";

    and "whoever murders shall be liable to judgment."

5:22 *But I say to you that if you are angry with a brother or sister,*

    you will be liable to judgment;

    and if you insult a brother or sister,

    you will be liable to the council;

    and if you say, "You fool,"

    you will be liable to the hell of fire.

5:23 *So when you are offering your gift at the altar,*

    if you remember

    that your brother or sister has something against you,

5:24 *leave your gift there before the altar and go;*

    first be reconciled to your brother or sister,

    and then come and offer your gift.

5:25 *Come to terms quickly with your accuser*

while you are on the way to court with him,

or your accuser may hand you over to the judge,

and the judge to the guard,

and you will be thrown into prison.

5:26 *Truly I tell you,*

you will never get out until you have paid the last penny.

GETTING INTO THE TEXT

This new section in the SM (5:17–48) concentrates on the type of "righteousness" or "justice" (Gr. *dikaiosynē*) that is to characterize the behavior of the members of Jesus' community as ones beckoned to follow God's way here on earth. According to 5:20, their righteousness is not to be tightfisted but abundant and overflowing, far surpassing that of the scribes and Pharisees. Beginning in 5:21–26, Jesus lays out six examples of how living by specific commandments of the Torah is to be understood generously rather than narrowly, in ways that promote healthy and honest relationships within the community and beyond.

In the first of what scholars call "the six antitheses" ("You have heard that it was said to those of ancient times . . . *but I say to you . . .*"), Jesus quotes "You shall not murder" in 5:21, a command familiar from the Decalogue (see Exod 20:13 and Deut 5:17). But the surprise comes in 5:22, where Jesus provides his interpretation of this prohibition. He appears to equate the crime of murder with a person's angry outbursts against a brother or sister in the community. Note the three-fold repetition in 5:22 where the offenses seem of equal seriousness while the corresponding penalties dramatically escalate. Everyone who is angry with another person in the community "will be liable to judgment" (Gr. *krisis*); and whoever says to a brother or sister, "You numskull" (Aramaic *Raca*)[1] will be liable to the Sanhedrin (the highest Jewish court); and whoever says, "You fool" (Gr. *mōron*) will be liable to the Gehenna of fire (eternal punishment).

---

1. *BDAG*, 903, states that *Raca*, a word derived from the Aramaic, is "a term of abuse/put-down relating to lack of intelligence, *numskull, fool* (in effect verbal bullying)."

It is noteworthy that the verbal form used for "are angry" in this verse occurs in the present tense, suggesting *continuing* and *simmering* anger, like nursing a grudge against the other person. Hence, the text is not proscribing a one-time angry outburst that arises spontaneously in reaction to a situation but rather long-term holding of hostile feelings towards a fellow Christian. Such smoldering anger easily erupts into verbal insults that demean and dismiss the other person, even though these abusive labels are often not taken all that seriously by the one who utters them.

Jesus, however, takes such dismissive language quite seriously. His intentional use of exaggerated rhetoric in 5:22 suggests he understands the destructive power of these abusive terms (*numskull* and *fool*). Jesus' heightened rhetoric seeks to grab the hearers' attention so they will confront the havoc that grudges and insults wreak within the life of the community. Nursing anger and name-calling are not innocuous; they hurt others and damage the communal spirit.

After Jesus' striking interpretation that connects murder with holding grudges, two examples in 5:23–26 are linked by "so" (meaning "therefore") to the previous section in 5:21–22, offering concrete illustrations of the need to channel the emotional energy of anger into the constructive activity of reconciliation.

The first illustration in 5:23–24 focuses on an individual person who, while offering a gift on the altar, recalls that a brother or sister in the community has something against the worshipper. The phrase "has something against you" seems intentionally vague, indicating neither the nature of the problem nor who is to blame. What hearers of the text do know is this: there is a rupture in the relationship between the one offering the gift at the altar and someone else in the community. Remembering this matter intrudes on a most sacred obligation, that of making an offering at the temple in Jerusalem. As Matthew's quoting of Hos 6:6a in 9:13 and 12:7 underlines ("I desire mercy, not sacrifice"), merciful activities in the community can even take precedence over worship activities. There might even be a playful exaggeration involved in Jesus' example if the original or later hearers of this text lived in Galilee at considerable distance from the Jerusalem temple. Leaving a gift in the temple, journeying home to Galilee and then back to Jerusalem, could easily require a week's travel. Hence, Jesus' call for reconciliation takes precedence and entails significant time.

The second concrete illustration in 5:25–26 entreats a person to become reconciled to an adversary in a lawsuit while accompanying that accuser on the way to court. Jesus thus urges control of anger and even making friends with the opponent in order to avoid the serious consequences of an appearance before a judge—imprisonment and demand for payment in full, the latter difficult to accomplish while in jail.

KNOWING THE CULTURAL CONTEXT

Jesus' warning about anger was originally directed to his Galilean followers, who lived in agrarian village communities, where interpersonal conflicts could have easily erupted in their daily face-to-face interactions. The text's mention of "brother or sister" (Gr. *adelphos* in 5:22) might initially have referred to one's neighbor in such a village community. By the late first century, however, when Matthew incorporates this saying on anger into his Gospel, Jesus' words also address conflicts among brothers and sisters in small Christian communities in an urban context. Close-knit communities need to maintain social order and harmony to exist and function.

Jesus' second illustration in 5:25–26 pictures a situation where one peasant villager owes a small debt to another who needs to be repaid (see also Luke 12:58–59). In this context, failure to act as friends and come to some arrangement would jeopardize the debtor's family and have larger repercussions within village relationships. In a similar situation in 1 Cor 6:1–8, Paul argues that the church-community in Corinth has its own wise leaders who should be able to arbitrate disputes between Christian brothers or sisters rather than involve non-Christian judges. The disharmony within the faith community projects an appalling witness to the larger society.

In the Jewish tradition itself, certain Proverbs demonstrate awareness of the destructive power of angry words or quick-tempered acts: "Whoever is slow to anger has great understanding, but the one who has a hasty temper exalts folly" (Prov 14:29), or "A soft answer turns away wrath, but a harsh word stirs up anger" (Prov 15:1). It is the fool who does not control his anger (see Prov 12:16, 12:18, and 14:17).

Finally, note that the full passage from which Jesus quotes the second great commandment ("You shall love your neighbor as yourself" in Matt 22:36–40) warns against seeking revenge or bearing grudges: "You shall not hate in your heart anyone of your kin; you shall reprove your neighbor, or you will incur guilt yourself. You shall not take vengeance or bear a grudge against any of your people, but you shall love your neighbor as yourself: I am the Lord" (Lev 19:17–18). Note that the passage urges the constructive action of "reproving" as a way to avoid taking revenge. Verbally confronting the neighbor can be an expression of love.[2] Not only are vengeance and grudges damaging to community, but they also are contrary to Jesus' vision of the rule of God.

ENGAGING THE TEXT TODAY

These words of Jesus are often misunderstood in present times. It is assumed that Jesus is forbidding angry feelings. Psychologists inform us that anger is a basic human emotion not simply banished by rational thoughts. In fact, anger can be a healthy response in situations of loss and grief or where injustice occurs. It is also the normal reaction to insult. Just recall your emotional reaction to another driver who cuts in front of you perilously or who makes an obscene gesture at you while overtaking your vehicle.

The purpose of Jesus' words in 5:22 was not to deny spontaneous anger but to remind us that our failure to deal constructively with anger causes serious damage to ourselves and community. In fact, nursing grudges and resentments can easily lead to contempt for the other person and result in verbal attacks on that person. The prevalence of name-calling in today's society in person or on the internet is perhaps at epidemic levels. The list of nasty and demeaning labels is long.

Insults to a person predictably trigger feelings of shame and intense rage that can erupt in violent and destructive ways or smolder beneath the surface. The old adage, "Sticks and stones can break my bones, but words can never hurt me" is patently false. Words—particularly when they attack a person's sense of identity and self-worth—take their toll on individuals, communities, and societies. The societal cost can be long-lasting. I recall a study, done some decades ago, that documented the

---

2. Milgrom, *Leviticus 17–22*, 1648, writes: "The opposite of hating in the heart is reproving in the open (i.e., to his face), a point that is indeed underscored in Prov 27:5 ['Better is open rebuke than hidden love'] . . . One of the ways to love your fellow, according to this unit (vv. 17–18), is to reprove him openly for his mistakes. And, conversely, the only admissible rebuke is that which is evoked by love, not by animosity, jealousy, or lust for power . . ."

effects of racist labels on young black children. The researcher requested every child in a racially mixed class to draw a picture of its classroom showing itself and the other children. The white children drew themselves as large and full figures in the picture. The black children, however, drew their white classmates as robust figures but themselves as diminutive and insignificant ones in the picture. Hearing "nigger" and other contemptuous terms directed at their parents and themselves over the years directly affected how they imaged themselves.

We can test this dynamic in light of our own experience. Remember past hurts, particularly when another person unmercifully ridiculed you for being overweight or not good at speaking or having a pimply face, or even worse, of being repeatedly humiliated as "dumb" or "stupid" by a parent or teacher. Simply recalling earlier experiences of belittling, especially if constant in early life, can resurface intense feelings in us—feelings of disgrace and shame and or even a sensation of rage.

In a family or congregation, grudges and name-calling can set off a nasty cycle of insults and even violence, rather than a circle of care and respect. Such insults have created long-lasting rifts and even warring factions that not only do irreparable harm to the community itself but also undermine that congregation's witness within the larger society. This is why Jesus surprisingly elevates unchecked anger to the level of murder. Nursed and rehearsed, anger can result in murder, but even far short of such a horrendous outcome, it can shatter a community of faith. Jesus' words in 5:21–26 do not deny that we frequently become angry and upset with one another in community. Rather, these words are calling us to find responsible and respectful ways to handle such angry feelings so that contempt and caustic comments find no lasting home within the life of the Christian community.

DWELLING IN THE TEXT

Quotes:

- Jesus is saying, then, that murder really begins when one loses his respect for human personality and the infinite worth of every individual. When a man spits in the face of his brother and looks with contempt upon him because of his race or some other fictitious difference, he has in his heart a spirit which may result in murder . . .

When one says "nigger," or "wop," or "chink," he is more of a murderer than he realizes.[3]

- "When you harbor a grudge, it is like drinking poison and expecting the other person to die."[4]

- "For he who gives no fuel to fire puts it out, and likewise he who does not in the beginning nurse his wrath and does not puff himself up with anger takes precautions against it and destroys it."[5]

Questions:

If the Bible study session is less than an hour, it is best to use only the starred questions. The mutual invitation process may be utilized when appropriate (see Appendix, page 156).

Focus on 5:21–22

*What is Jesus saying about anger? How can anger be as serious as murder?

How would these words of Jesus impact the first-century hearers?

What makes you angry?

*How does anger turn into a grudge?

In what way does harboring anger affect the angry person?

What are examples of nasty epithets used today in our society?

Can you remember an instance when in anger you called another person a nasty name?

How did this name-calling make you feel?

---

3. Jordan, *Sermon*, 55–56.

4. This saying was shared by a participant in the St. Mark Center Brown Bag Ecumenical Bible Study in Dubuque, IA.

5. Plutarch, as quoted in Tavris, *Anger*, 131.

Focus on 5:23–26

*Can you offer an example where grudges and name-calling harmed a congregation?

How do Jesus' examples in 5:23–26 offer us guidance as we deal with anger in our congregation?

*Is Jesus' teaching good or bad therapy? Why?

How can a church-community deal constructively with anger?

*How does the story of Jesus' crucifixion and resurrection address our problem of anger?

Exercises:

1) In pairs, share a time when someone called you a nasty name. What was the abusive label (if you are willing to share), and how did being labeled make you feel? Make sure that both persons have opportunity to share.

2) Give each person a pencil and a piece of paper. Take the group into the worship area of the church building to be in the presence of the altar. Instruct them to offer a gift (imaginary or real) at the altar, and then have them interrupt that process as they remember someone with whom they are at odds. Participants should go away from the altar (leaving their gift there) and take time to compose a dialogue with the other party against whom they hold ill feelings. Instruct participants to draw a line down the middle of their paper, writing down on the one side what they would ask the adversary. Next, they should write down on the other side what the other person would say in response. Continue the dialogue on paper by writing what would be said next, followed by its rebuttal, and so on. Each participant should use about fifteen to twenty minutes to develop the imagined dialogue with the other person. When done, the participants will return to the altar and re-offer their gifts. Finally, reassemble the group for a brief discussion on what the participants have learned about the biblical passage and themselves by doing this exercise. Close with prayer and sharing the peace.

3) Have the group members sit in a circle. Instruct the participants to stand and shout out any invectives or nasty names used to demean other people (e.g., dummy, slut, nigger, shit). Encourage them to shout out the derogatory names randomly and even if others are shouting at

the time. After a few minutes of doing this, ask everyone to stop and be seated. After some silence invite them to think of names bestowed (by God) on others in the community of faith. Bid them to call out gently all the names God would have us employ in addressing one another (e.g., child of God, sister, beloved one, brother).

Songs:

"God, When Human Bonds Are Broken" (ELW, 603; HFTG, 155; WOV, 735; W&R, 416)

"At The Altar" (BC, 2:551)

"Go, My Children, with My Blessing" (ELW, 543; GTG, 547; TNCH, 82; W&R, 719).

"Oh, Praise the Gracious Power" (TPH, 471; WOV, 750)—especially verses 1 and 2

"What Have We to Offer?" (W&P, 156)

"Not for Tongues of Heaven's Angels" (W&R, 400)

Prayers:

O Compassionate God, you have mercifully absorbed the worst of human anger and rage in the crucifixion of Jesus. Free us daily from any contempt we might harbor towards others, and help us to risk taking steps of reconciliation towards those with whom we feel at odds. For Jesus' sake. Amen.

Or you may choose to use the prayer circle to close your session (see Appendix, page 159).

5

Blessed Community
—Challenged to Value Women

LUST (MATTHEW 5:27-30)

5:27 *You have heard that it was said,*

    "You shall not commit adultery."

5:28 *But I say to you*

    that everyone who looks at a woman with lust

        has already committed adultery with her in his heart.

5:29 *If your right eye causes you to sin, tear it out and throw it away;*

    it is better for you to lose one of your members

        than for your whole body to be thrown into hell.

5:30 *And if your right hand causes you to sin,*

    cut it off and throw it away;

    it is better for you to lose one of your members

        than for your whole body to go into hell.

DIVORCE (MATTHEW 5:31-32)

5:31 *It was also said,*

> "Whoever divorces his wife,
>
> let him give her a certificate of divorce."
>
> 5:32 But I say to you that anyone who divorces his wife,
>
> except on the ground of unchastity,
>
> causes her to commit adultery;
>
> and whoever marries a divorced woman commits adultery.

GETTING INTO THE TEXT

In this chapter, we consider the next two antitheses together since they both concern how men treated women in the biblical world. These hard sayings of Jesus were directed to men since they had controlling power in gender and family relationships. Contemporary relationships between men and women can be quite different.

The overall pattern for 5:27–30 is quite similar to the previous text, but now Jesus quotes in 5:27 the Decalogue's prohibition against adultery (Exod 20:14 and Deut 5:18). Jesus' interpretation of the commandment again invites more than mere compliance with the letter of the law. The surprise this time is his equating a man's deliberate lustful gaze towards another man's wife with adultery. The Greek word *gynē* in 5:28 likely implies a married woman. It is not merely an innocent glance. He craves to have her sexually. When this occurs, Jesus states, "he has already committed adultery with her in his heart." Since in biblical understanding "heart" represents the inner thinking, feeling, and volition of a person, Jesus is implying that such an adulterous intent gains a foothold in the core of that person.

By using exaggeration, the two examples that follow in 5:29–30 are shocking and underscore the seriousness of unbridled lust. The text's reference to "eye" and "hand" alludes respectively to the man's capacity to "see" the woman and then "act" upon his ensuing desire.[1] Mentioning explicitly "*right* eye" and "*right* hand" suggests that it is preferable to lose one's *better* body parts than to lose one's whole person to Gehenna, the place of judgment. Because it is literally possible to tear out one's right eye or actually to cut off one's right hand, these two examples have

---

1. See Malina and Rohrbaugh, *Commentary,* 419–20, for a brief description of the "Three-Zone Personality."

enormous rhetorical power and cannot be dismissed easily by hearers as mere figurative speech. Jesus' imaginative language intends to stun and alarm those who view a man's sexual appetite for another's wife as natural and fairly harmless.

Jesus' saying about divorce in 5:31–32 makes a logical connection with the previous passage. Lust for another man's wife becomes a major cause of divorce. Jesus disturbingly ties both a man's lustful appetite for another's wife and a man's divorce of his own wife to the act of adultery. Even as it is a grave matter to contribute in any way to the breakup of someone else's marriage, it is equally serious to terminate one's own marriage.

The structure of this brief text is straightforward. After the introductory formula ("It was also said"), there is a paraphrase in verse 31 of a scriptural passage stipulating conditions for remarriage of a divorced woman (cf. Deut 24:1–4). Then 5:32 advances Jesus' interpretation ("But I say to you") in two parallel statements. It is important to note that the primary intent of Deut 24:1–4 is to prevent a man from reclaiming a former wife once he has divorced her and another man has married her. Even if a second or third husband should subsequently divorce the woman, it would be "abhorrent to the Lord" for her first husband to reclaim her as his wife. Written from a male perspective, the passage reads, "Suppose a man enters into marriage with a woman, but she does not please him because he finds *something objectionable about her*, and so he writes her a certificate of divorce, puts it in her hand, and sends her out of his house . . ." (Deut 24:1, italics mine). This passage presents a simple procedure for divorce and assumes the husband's prerogative to issue the divorce document.

Jesus' treatment of Deut 24:1–4, linking divorce to adultery, challenges its basic assumption that a man has a right to divorce his wife. Jesus' first declaration in 5:32 names the consequence of divorce for the wife—it causes her to become an adulteress. This is puzzling since divorce within the Jewish world was intended to make remarriage possible for the divorced woman. Jesus' interpretation seems to make remarriage more difficult, if not impossible. Was Jesus meaning that on the basis of God's original intention for marriage nothing should interrupt or adulterate that bond, not even the husband's right of divorce? In biblical society, the divorced wife was placed in an impossible position. In the eyes of most, she would appear as an adulteress, as one who had been sexually unfaithful to her husband, even if that was not in fact the case. She would also become extremely vulnerable in that society since a woman needed to be under the care of a man—husband, father, or brother—for support and protection. According to Jesus, however, by remarrying she enters an adulterous relationship since the first marriage remains valid.

Jesus' second declaration in 5:32b ("and whoever marries a divorced woman commits adultery") has implications for other men. One scholar states, "The prohibition of marriage to a divorced woman extends the Old Testament prohibition of the husband marrying his own divorced wife a second time (Deut 24:4) to all divorced women."[2] These words seem a contrast to Jesus' demonstrated kindness towards women, unless it is understood that these words are addressed to married men who should not divorce their wives.

There is yet one other matter to mention. As Jesus' approach to Deut 24:1–4 is stated in 5:32, there is an exception: "anyone who divorces his wife, except on the ground of unchastity, causes her to commit adultery." This phrase about the exception that includes the word *porneia*, a general term in Greek for sexual immorality, has been much discussed and can imply various situations. In this instance, it likely refers to a wife's infidelity, which would be tantamount to adultery. Since this same exception is also included in Matt 19:3–12, a longer story prompted by the Pharisees' question about divorce, and not in Mark 10:2–12, it seems probable that it has been added by the author of Matthew to interpret Jesus' saying to his church-communities in the late first century. Moreover, many scholars deduce that Jesus' comment about divorce and remarriage was not intended as a legal ruling but as a principle to be interpreted flexibly. The culminating saying in the Markan story states "Therefore what God has joined together, let no one separate" (Mark 10:9). This saying, not formulated as a legal command that categorically forbids divorce, intends to illuminate the importance of the marriage relationship.

What, then, do the words of Jesus in 5:27–30 and 5:31–32 imply for Matthew's faith communities? Their challenge to the men within the communities is plain and dramatic. Jesus acknowledges the power of sexual lust in men and shows its seriousness by equating lusting to adultery. He also challenges the presumed right to divorce a wife by advocating the permanence of the marriage covenant, which is made even clearer in Mark 10:2–9 where he appeals to God's intention for marriage from creation and labels the use of Deut 24:1–4 as a divine concession

2. Luz, *Matthew*, 307.

to human sin. Finally, both antitheses make sense as part of Jesus' call in the SM for a "better righteousness" (see 5:20). The men of the Christian community are not permitted divorce as a right, and the women are not offered the protection of remarriage. Rather, men are challenged to take with utter seriousness the marital relationship in which they participate. A later text in Matt 19:10–12 implies that some men viewed Jesus' saying about divorce so difficult that they preferred not to marry. That text, as well as Paul's words in 1 Cor 7:7, offers evidence that some early Christians chose the celibate life for the sake of kingdom work rather than marriage. Christian communities took marriage so seriously they came to value celibacy as well.

KNOWING THE CULTURAL CONTEXT

A few more details about the first-century cultural context help us to appreciate the import of these texts featuring men's treatment of women.

First, it is important to recognize that in the ancient world marriages were usually arranged, linking the honor and well-being of two extended families, and had little or nothing to do with choice—particularly of the woman. The woman would leave her father's family and be incorporated into her new husband's household. Often the woman was considerably younger than her husband. Our romantic notion of falling in love and choosing to marry would be quite foreign to this first-century world.

Second, it is necessary to clarify the meaning of *adultery* in the Jewish world. Simply put, adultery is sexual intercourse between a married (or engaged) woman and any man other than the woman's husband. It is another man violating, or adulterating, a husband's relationship with his wife—a sin seen primarily as an offense against the husband himself. The seriousness of this offense is signaled by the death penalty for both the woman and the male interloper (see Lev 20:10 and Deut 22:22), although there is little evidence that this penalty was actually enforced during Jesus' time. Adultery was a grave sin since it could introduce confusion about the purity of the husband's progeny.

Third, more needs to be said about the lively debate at the time of Jesus, and beyond, regarding the legal reason permitting a man to divorce his wife—the question the Pharisees posed to Jesus in Matt 19:3. This debate among Jewish teachers, or rabbis, focused on the ambiguous phrase in Deut 24:1—"something objectionable about her" (Hebrew 'erwat dabar). The Mishnah, the written record of these debates about the proper understanding of Torah commandments, preserves differing conclusions by prominent rabbis just before the time of Jesus regarding the phrase "something objectionable." The school of Rabbi Shammai argued for a narrow understanding as a reference to the wife's adulterous act, whereas the school of Rabbi Hillel offered a much more lenient reading of the phrase, stating that a man had grounds for divorcing his wife even if she spoiled his meal.[3] This rabbinic dispute is apparently the larger cultural and religious context for the Pharisee's query of Jesus, an argument that continued into the time of the Matthean church communities. These communities evidently had to defend Jesus' interpretation of the Jewish Law in light of accusations by their synagogue leaders (see 5:17–20).

The final topic is the place and role of women in the first-century Mediterranean world. Women were typically viewed as weaker and softer than men—less controlled, more fearful, petty, irrational, and emotional. The household, not the public arena, was the primary sphere where women existed and functioned, although poorer village women were also active in fieldwork. Given some uncomplimentary statements about women at that time, it is striking that no negative sayings regarding women are attributed to Jesus in the Gospel tradition. Rather, Jesus healed women on more than one occasion (e.g., Mark 1:29–31, Mark 5:21–43,and Luke 13:10–17). Contrary to the behavior of other rabbis, he associated with them in public and even had some women in the wider circle of his disciples, with a few serving him and providing material support out of their resources (Mark 15:40–41 and Luke 8:1–3). Women were significant and valued members of the church-communities addressed by Matthew's Gospel. In the SM, Jesus is concerned about relationships between men and women as integral to the *ecology of relationships* rooted in the righteousness that is generated by God's merciful and lavish love (see 5:20).

ENGAGING THE TEXT TODAY

Though these tough sayings of Jesus targeted only the men of his day, our changed situation suggests that women need to take them seriously as well, since they too have the same opportunity to break up a marriage.

---

3. See the Mishnah, *Gittin*, 9:10.

Clearly today, sexual misconduct by both men and women can easily damage a Christian congregation. According to my colleague Dan Olson, lust and divorce, like anger, can be linked to *contempt* for the other person. If lust is viewed as only having to do with the interior desire and feelings of a person, then the word of Jesus could be seen as a proscription of these sexual feelings. We all have heard of well-known evangelists who warned of the sinfulness of lustful thoughts. This can lead an individual to attempt to deny sexual feelings, rather than recognizing that Jesus is addressing our need to acknowledge these feelings and control them through respect for others and concern for the community's well-being. Since we do have sexual feelings, we need to deal with them responsibly.

Some psychologists draw a distinction between *lust* and *love*. Love involves relating to another human being *as a person*. Lust involves dealing with the other *as a thing*. When a man, for example, views a woman as a sexual object, he can use her to satisfy his own desire with little consideration for her personhood. Rape is an extreme form of viewing the other merely as a sex object to be used and abused.

Our American society, which commercializes sex and exploits lust, is a challenging environment for Christians. Pornography is a multi-billion dollar business. Movies and TV series routinely flaunt sexual escapades involving married persons with no attention to the human consequences of such affairs. Studies show that women who have affairs often deal with negative results, including high levels of anxiety and unhappiness. Most media, however, never reveal these consequences.

Our current society seems to tolerate adultery and divorce. In a context where over 40 percent of marriages end in divorce, many people have become wary of long-term relationships and are reluctant to commit to another person. Marriage can be seen as a curb on one's freedom or as a harbinger of unhappiness. All this overlooks the enriching role of marriage for individuals and community, for without commitment, trust is undermined.

In 5:27–30, the concern is that lust will lead to adultery. The church-communities addressed by Matthew's Gospel encouraged mutuality and equal participation in the fellowship between both men *and* women, a reality we know today. With this increased social interaction came possibilities for more sexual carelessness, leading to divorce and disruption within families and the larger community of faith. Though our society does not seem to agree with the hyperbolic words of Jesus in 5:27–32, it is important that Christian communities take his words seriously. More than ever, pastoral leaders and lay people need to be talking about human sexuality and how healthy communities deal with these powerful feelings that we human beings experience.

DWELLING IN THE TEXT

Quotes:

- We live in various relationships, all of which are affected by the physiological, psychological, and social aspects of our sexual identity. People of all ages need information and experience to understand and responsibly live out their sexual identity in the varied relationships of their lives—as child or parent, sister or brother, spouse, friend, co-worker, neighbor, or stranger. This church affirms the importance of ordering society and educating youth and adults so that all might live in these relationships with mutual respect and responsibility.[4]

- Sexual violence statistics:[5]

  - Every two minutes, someone in the U.S. is sexually assaulted.

  - One in six women and one in thirty-three men will be victims of sexual assault in their lifetimes.

  - Sixty percent of sexual assaults are not reported to the police.

  - Approximately 73 percent of rape victims know their assailants.

Questions:

If the Bible study session is less than an hour, it is best to use only the starred questions. To ensure everyone's participation at critical points in the discussion, utilize the process of mutual invitation (see Appendix, page 156).

Focus on 5:27–30

*What is Jesus saying about lust in this text?

4. "Sexuality: Some Common Convictions," ELCA Statement, 1996.

5. These statistics and more are presented on the website for Faith Trust Institute, whose founder is the Rev. Dr. Marie M. Fortune. See www.faithtrustinstitute.org.

*How does lusting affect relationships between men and women?

⟶ How are verbal abuse (5:21–26) and sexual abuse (5:27–30) connected?

*How is lust a problem for men today in our society?

*Is lust also a problem for women in our society? Why or why not?

Focus on 5:31–32

*In what way is Jesus' concern about divorce in his patriarchal society still relevant in our more egalitarian situation today?

How does your congregation help members value marriage as a commitment before God and important to its life and mission?

How does your congregation help men to value women? And vice versa?

How are the experiences and needs of divorced persons acknowledged in your congregation?

Focus on 5:27–30 and 5:31–32

What is your faith community doing to address important matters of sexuality? What more could it be doing?

In what ways does our highly sexualized culture present challenges to your congregation's youth in high school, college, and work places?

*Are Jesus' challenging words in any sense "good news" for us? Why or why not?

Exercises:

1) In small groups, discuss one or more of the following questions: *How challenging is it to be a single person in this culture? How challenging is it to be a married person? How challenging is it to be a divorced person?* After about fifteen minutes for sharing in pairs, invite the entire group to respond to the following question: *What did you learn from this time of sharing?*

2) For use at the beginning of the session: The leader should select a portion of a current movie or TV program, portraying adults involved

in adulterous relationships with no attention to the consequences of their actions. At the start of the session, have the group participants view the prepared segment and then offer briefly their initial reactions to the scene. Then, have the group do a study of the text. At the end of the session revisit the video clip, allowing time for further reflection.

Songs:

"Great God, Your Love Has Called Us" (ELW, 358; TPH, 353; W&R, 55—can use tune Ryburn)

"God, When Human Bonds Are Broken" (ELW, 603; HFTG, 155; WOV, 735; W&R, 416)

"Our Father, We Have Wandered" (ELW, 606; WOV, 733; W&R, 371)

"Come Down, O Love Divine" (ELW, 804; GTG, 282; TNCH, 289; TPH, 313; TH1982, 516; W&R, 330)

"Love Divine, All Loves Excelling" (ELW, 631; GTG, 366; LBW, 315; TH1982, 657; TNCH, 43; TPH, 376; TUMH, 384; W&R, 358)

Prayers:

O gracious God, you have created us as sexual beings. Make us gentle and kind with each other. Give us truthfulness in our closest relationships and the wisdom to seek counsel and care when we are hurting and in need. Strengthen our congregation as a community of healthy interaction between women and men. Make us a place of safety for all our youth. This we ask in the name of Jesus, who shared our humanity. Amen.

You may also choose to use the prayer circle to close your session (see Appendix, page 159).

6

Blessed Community
—Trusted Truth-Tellers

MATTHEW 5:33-37

5:33 *Again, you have heard that it was said to those of ancient times,*

"*You shall not swear falsely,*

but carry out the vows you have made to the Lord."

5:34 *But I say to you,*

Do not swear at all,

either   by heaven,   *for it is the throne of God,*

5:35   or   by the earth,   *for it is his footstool,*

or   by Jerusalem,   *for it is the city of the great King.*

5:36 *And do not swear*

by your head,   *for you cannot make one hair*

white or black.

5:37 *Let your word be 'Yes, Yes' or 'No, No';*

anything more than this comes from the evil one."

GETTING INTO THE TEXT

This text focuses on the prohibition "You shall not swear falsely . . ." (5:33). Although these words are not a direct scriptural quote, the warning is well attested in the Hebrew Scripture and certainly relates to the commandment regarding bearing false witness against a neighbor (Exod 20:16 and Deut 5:20). But it also concerns the second commandment (Exod 20:7), since oath-taking normally involved invoking the name of God. Lev 19:12 refers to such a blasphemous use of God's name—"And you shall not swear falsely *by my name*, profaning the name of your God: I am the Lord."

The final portion of 5:33 ("but carry out the vows you have made to the Lord") underscores the importance of keeping a vow made before God—a promise of a particular offering or action. Elsewhere, Deut 23:21–23 states: "If you make a vow to the Lord your God, do not postpone fulfilling it; for the Lord your God will surely require it of you, and you would incur guilt. But if you refrain from vowing, you will not incur guilt. Whatever your lips utter you must diligently perform, just as you have freely vowed to the Lord your God with your own mouth."

Because biblical societies relied heavily on oral exchanges to survive and prosper, the highest value was placed on the trustworthiness of a person's words. It was not always easy, however, to discern whether or not another person's affirmation or denial was true or false, especially if that person was not a close associate or kin. For this reason, oath-taking became a form of speech appealing to a higher authority to vouch for a person's truthfulness. It was assumed that failure to keep an oath would bring that person negative consequences from the Deity. Thus the biblical people viewed such oaths as the indispensable guarantee of honesty in human speech. These oaths were needed to minimize disputes as Heb 6:16 implies: "Human beings, of course, swear by someone greater than themselves, and an oath given as confirmation puts an end to all dispute."

By the time the Gospel of Matthew was written (about 75–85 CE), blatant disregard for honoring oaths (as well as their overuse) had become problematic. A later passage in Matthew points to nuanced debates among Jewish leaders regarding what in fact constituted a binding oath (see 23:16–22). That oaths were used for trifling matters and evidently got out of hand is suggested by the dedication of an entire section to defining and certifying oaths in the Mishnah, the written version of the oral discussion about the Torah.[1]

In 5:34–37, Jesus does not simply prohibit *false* swearing, but categorically rejects all use of oaths, much as did a group called the Essenes that resided in a desert community at Qumran along the Dead Sea.[2] Jesus invites straightforward honesty in speech so that no outside validation is needed. In 5:34–36, Jesus bolsters his unambiguous proscription of oath-taking by four examples of commonly used oaths. In each case, a reason supports the prohibition. The sequence of places by which a person guarantees his oath moves from the distant "heaven" to "earth" and then to "Jerusalem" and finally to what is closest to the oath-maker—his own "head." The first three are ways to invoke God without direct use of the divine name (see Isa 66:1 and Ps 48:1–2). As with the first three, the final one—swearing by one's head—was also thought to be a domain over which the oath-taker had no control.

This text in the SM ends with Jesus' positive directive to his community: "Let your word be 'Yes, Yes' or 'No, No'; anything more than this comes from the evil one" (see also Jas 5:12). Jesus invites the community of his followers to plain honesty in speech. The doubling of the "yes" and "no" does not create a new oath but simply underscores the importance of their non-deceptive use of words. For Matthew's audience, in light of the legalistic practices described in 23:16–22, Jesus' call for straightforward and truthful use of words was refreshing. All the distinctions and qualifications surrounding oath-taking, determining which ones a person was obligated to keep and which ones might be ignored, could easily become the enemy of speaking the truth.

Truthfulness in speech is thus being recommended for its own sake and for the good of the community. Truth-telling is an integral part of the *better righteousness* Jesus commended (see 5:20), essential for building trust within the community of faith. Uttering words with intent to deceive, on the contrary, quickly undermines trust and threatens the harmony of the community. Life together in a SM community requires

---

1. See *Shabuot* in the Mishnah.

2. Josephus, *Jewish War*, 2:8:6, writes of the Essenes: "Holding righteous indignation in reserve, they are masters of their temper, champions of fidelity, very ministers of peace. *Any word of theirs has more force than an oath; swearing they avoid, regarding it as worse than perjury, for they say that one who is not believed without an appeal to God stands condemned already*" (italics mine).

honest speech among its members for its own well-being and for the integrity of its witness to the larger society.

KNOWING THE CULTURAL CONTEXT

It is almost impossible for us to imagine a culture that does not depend heavily on the printed word, whether on paper or conveyed electronically. The first-century Roman world, however, was primarily an oral culture, with approximately 90 percent of the population unable to read or write. Those few who had enough formal education to do so, such as the scribes in the Gospels, exercised considerable authority because they could read earlier sacred writings and could create other written documents. But it is crucial to understand that what was written was done in order to be read and heard by a far larger number of people. The biblical culture's reliance on oral speech was primary and foundational.

The spoken word was viewed as powerful and able to achieve what it promised. This was true for not only divine words but also human ones. It is significant that in Hebrew the term *dabar* has a range of meanings including "word" or "speech," as well as "event" or "happening" (see, e.g., Isa 55:10–11). Hence, the utterance of blessings and curses was viewed not just as "words" but also as "events" to be taken with the utmost seriousness, as were oaths and vows. Failure to honor one's verbal promises or intentionally deceiving others tore at the social fabric of the community.

Some passages in the Hebrew Scriptures clearly point to the problem of people not taking their oaths seriously. Certain prophets, for example, attacked this abuse of oaths: "Yes, thus says the Lord God: I will deal with you as you have done, you who have despised the oath, breaking the covenant" (Ezek 16:59), and "These are the things that you shall do: Speak the truth to one another, render in your gates judgments that are true and make for peace, do not devise evil in your hearts against one another, and love no false oath; for all these are things that I hate, says the Lord" (Zech 8:16–17). As a final example, a Jewish document written in the second century BCE directly confronts the overuse of oaths.

> Do not accustom your mouth to oaths,
> nor habitually utter the name of the Holy One;
> for as a servant who is constantly under scrutiny
> will not lack bruises,
> so also the person who always swears and utters the Name
> will never be cleansed from sin.

> The one who swears many oaths is full of iniquity,
> and the scourge will not leave his house.
> If he swears in error, his sin remains on him,
> and if he disregards it, he sins doubly;
> if he swears a false oath, he will not be justified,
> for his house will be filled with calamities (Sir 23:9–11).

By the first century CE, such overuse and even abuse of the verbal oath evidently led to ongoing debate among Jewish teachers regarding when one must keep the oath made. Jesus directed harsh words at the scribes and Pharisees in Matt 23:16–22:

> Woe to you, blind guides, who say,
> "Whoever swears by the sanctuary is bound by nothing,
> but whoever swears by the gold of the sanctuary
> is bound by the oath."
> You blind fools!
> For which is greater,
> the gold or the sanctuary that has made the gold sacred?
> And you say,
> "Whoever swears by the altar is bound by nothing,
> but whoever swears by the gift that is on the altar
> is bound by the oath."
> How blind you are!
> For which is greater,
> the gift or the altar that makes the gift sacred?
> So whoever swears by the altar,
> swears by it and by everything on it;
> and whoever swears by the sanctuary,
> swears by it and by the one who dwells in it;
> and whoever swears by heaven,
> swears by the throne of God
> and by the one who is seated upon it.

ENGAGING THE TEXT TODAY

Unlike the biblical world, there are too few communities in American society where "giving one's word" is expected or taken seriously. We have become suspicious of public promises since words are often used deceptively. This dishonesty has resulted in the legal system playing an exaggerated role in our society. Some people will only speak the truth if made to do so under oath, although even this does not always guarantee that lying is precluded.

It seems that increasing numbers of people in our society feel no compulsion to tell the truth because they do not take seriously God as the guardian of truth. Our situation is worse than in Jesus' day since the problem is more than profaning the name of God. Many do not consider God at all. What they say is a matter of expediency and to their personal advantage.

We humans have an enormous capacity to use speech to delude others and ourselves. This deception can involve the seemingly innocent flattery of another person, when actually feeling disgust. Or it can be deliberate lying. A field of psychology known as "impression management" attempts to investigate the multiple ways we use speech deceptively to make the right impression. This tendency is exacerbated by internet social networks that invite a person to fashion his or her "personal profile." In the process we can alter the truth, presenting ourselves to be more attractive, more talented, or more honest than in fact we are. Deceptive use of language also occurs on the societal level, for example, in advertising and political campaigning. We sometimes hold little confidence that candidates are really honest in the promises they make to get elected.

Our contemporary society is quite different from the biblical world that relied on the veracity of the spoken word of people. Today we have electronic technologies to record past conversations and statements. We can prove what was said and done in the past. Yet our technological capacity often appears to complicate the search for truth, since this technology in no way guarantees that people will speak honestly.

The more words a society churns out, the more speech is cheapened and the more deception there can be. Jesus goes to the basics: simply tell the truth. The intent to deceive very quickly undermines trust among people in a community. One researcher on lying alerts us to the massive danger of lying in society or community: "These practices [of lying and deceptive speech] clearly do not affect only isolated individuals. The veneer of social trust is often thin. As lies spread—by imitation, or in retaliation, or to forestall suspected deception—trust is damaged. Yet trust is a social good to be protected just as much as the air we breathe or the water we drink. When it is damaged, the community as a whole suffers, and when it is destroyed, societies falter and collapse."[3]

3. Bok, *Lying*, 26–27.

Jesus' clarion call for simple truth-speaking is critical for Christian congregations. The more the larger society is threatened by untruthful speech, the more urgent it is for communities of faith to behave quite differently in how and why they say "yes" and "no." A Christian community can provide a powerful contrast, and thus witness, to the larger society as a gathering place where people learn to trust what others say. For Christians, such trust is ultimately rooted in the Triune God, who is the guarantor of truth and the judge of all deception. More than that, simple telling of the truth is far easier than even the smallest scheme of deception. It is refreshing to be around others who tell the truth. Such honesty helps relationships to flourish and community to be built up.

DWELLING IN THE TEXT

Quotes:

- "I've learned that people usually tell you the truth if you listen hard enough. If you don't, you'll hear what they think you want to hear."[4]

- "If you tell the truth, you don't have to remember anything."[5]

- "When regard for truth has been broken down or even highly weakened, all things will remain doubtful."[6]

- "Truth speaking demands willingness to sacrifice and is framed in a context of risk—the risk of defeat, taken for the sake of the truth."[7]

Questions:

The starred questions are suggested for sessions shorter than an hour:
   *What problems regarding oaths do you suppose this text is addressing?
   *Why do people take oaths?

---

4. Novogratz, *Sweater,* 273.

5. A saying attributed to Mark Twain (see www.ThinkExit.com)

6. A saying attributed Augustine, who wrote about lying.

7. Westhelle, *God,* 89.

*In what ways are deceptive words used in our society? In our congregation?

*What happens to people in a community when its participants use words deceitfully?

How does it feel personally to become the victim of another's deception or broken trust?

Why are we not always honest in what we say to other people?

How do we use language that is self-deluding?

What is involved in "speaking the truth in love" (cf. Eph 4:14–16)?

*What role can a community of faith play in restoring trust in the truthfulness of others?

How does your community of faith encourage honesty in speech?

What responsibility do we as individuals have for truth-telling?

Exercises:

1) In pairs, invite each person to be honest and share in confidence one example of an occasion when he or she offered a false reason for doing or not doing something and the after-effects. After each has shared, have each discuss his or her motivation for being deceptive. If you have time, ask the participants to share with the full group what they learned from this exercise.

2) Enlist three persons to do a role-play before the entire group. Have two of the volunteers leave the room, and then instruct the remaining person to fabricate two explanations why he or she had been absent from a church council meeting last week (or some other important gathering the person was expected to attend). Next, tell that person to relate one explanation to one of the two other persons (who comes into the room, hears the account, and leaves). Then the fabricator will use the other reason in explaining the absence to the second person who enters the room. Finally, invite all three individuals into the room and encourage them to talk with the one another about the council meeting (or another gathering) and why the one party had been absent. Determine how hard it is for the fabricator to keep from being trapped in his or her deceptive speech. An optional topic might be a husband explaining to his wife and teenage son why he failed to attend the school play as promised.

Songs:

> "Lord, Keep Us Steadfast in Your Word" (ELW, 517)
>
> "Take My Life, That I May Be" (ELW, 583, 685; GTG, 697; TNCH, 448; TPH, 391; TUMH, 399; TH1982, 707; W&R, 466)
>
> "Take Thou Our Minds, Dear Lord" (GTG, 707; TPH, 392; W&R, 455)
>
> "God, When Human Bonds Are Broken" (ELW, 603; HFTG, 155; WOV, 735; W&R, 416)

Prayers:

O God, you know us in ways we do not even know ourselves. Keep us from deceiving others and even ourselves. Help us to be honest in our words and reliable in our actions because of Jesus Christ, your trustworthy presence among us. Amen.

Or you may choose to close by using the prayer circle (see Appendix, page 159).

7

Blessed Community
—Risking Non-Violent Power

MATTHEW 5:38–42

5:38 *You have heard that it was said,*

"An eye for an eye and a tooth for a tooth."

5:39 *But I say to you,*

Do not resist an evildoer.

But if anyone strikes you on the right cheek,

turn the other also;

5:40 *and if anyone wants to sue you and take your coat,*

give your cloak as well;

5:41 *and if anyone forces you to go one mile,*

go also the second mile.

5:42 *Give to everyone who begs from you,*

and do not refuse anyone who wants to borrow from you.

GETTING INTO THE TEXT

"An eye for an eye and a tooth for a tooth" (5:38) offers an example of *lex talionis* or "the law of the talon" (referring to the claw of an animal or bird of prey). Lev 24:19–20 states, "Anyone who maims another shall suffer the same injury in return: fracture for fracture, eye for eye, tooth for tooth; the injury inflicted is the injury to be suffered" (cf. also Exod 21:22–25 and Deut 19:21). Contrary to our immediate impression, this legal principle had a salutary purpose—to limit revenge by matching the punishment to the crime. Without it, revenge-taking could easily escalate between the antagonistic parties. The party or group initially victimized invariably would inflict greater injury in retaliation, with the possibility that the cycle of violent payback spirals out of control.

Jesus' response, in 5:39–42, to this ancient legal formula is unexpected. He begins with what appears to be a general principle—"Do not resist an evildoer"—and then adds four illustrations of how this non-retaliatory principle might play out in concrete situations involving a slap on the face, loss of a garment in a court case, being pressed into service by a Roman soldier, and a request for help or a loan. In situations in which one would naturally react negatively or even retaliate, Jesus calls for alternative responses by his followers as befitting the *better righteousness* (5:20).

Much scholarly debate surrounds the four examples—what precisely was Jesus envisioning in each instance? In the well-known first one in 5:39b ("But if anyone strikes you on the right cheek, turn the other also"), notice that the *right* cheek is specifically mentioned, a detail missing in the parallel in Luke 6:29. This implies a back-of-hand blow by the right hand to the right check of the offended person, intended as an insult rather than designed to do actual physical harm. Such a strike would be an affront to a man's honor and thus a grave humiliation.

But how is Jesus' directive "turn the other cheek" to be understood? Is it simply an example of passive non-resistance, or does it involve something more? Walter Wink and others have argued that Jesus is here calling for an imaginative and even provocative way of reacting to such an insult.[1] It is not an action of someone who cowardly submits to the offender but represents taking the initiative and turning the tables on the perpetrator. *Turning the other cheek* puts the insulter in an awkward position, since for him to respond to the exposed left cheek requires either

---

1. Wink, *Engaging*, 175–77.

escalating the violence by delivering an open-handed blow with his right hand or committing a dishonorable act with the back of his left hand. The right hand was used for respectable acts such as eating and greeting others while the left hand was left for the unclean tasks of personal hygiene. The strict Jewish community living at Qumran by the Dead Sea even had a law against gesturing with the left hand in public meetings.[2]

Hence, the gesture of turning the other cheek not only avoids retaliating but also exposes the offense for what it is—culturally deplorable and unacceptable. For the offender to strike again would reveal that person as vulgar and uncivilized. This surprising response of turning the other cheek thus has the potential of transforming the thinking and action of the offender. (Try enacting this "turning the cheek" action to illustrate how it works!).

The second illustration (5:40) entails a court case involving an antagonist, likely a man of some means, demanding from a poor man his tunic or shirt (Gr. *chitōn* denotes the garment worn next to the skin) as payment for a debt. In response, Jesus says, "give your cloak as well." A poor person's cloak or robe (Gr. *himation*), according to Exod 22:25–27 and Deut 24:12–13, is his inalienable possession since it is needed as a cover for sleeping at night. Wink suggests that Jesus' directive to give the creditor the cloak as well is once more provocative. Imagine this: if the person from whom the shirt were demanded actually hands over his outer cloak, that person would be standing stark naked before his antagonist in the court. This nakedness would be an embarrassment to those present and especially to the one demanding his shirt. The adversary would have clearly pushed matters too far. As with the first example, the act of giving up the cloak dramatically changes the character of the scene. Now the one who insists on payment is put on the defensive and must rethink his action.[3]

The third illustration in 5:41 imagines a situation of enforced service. The Greek verb *aggareuein* refers to service demanded of someone by an official or soldier with power to enforce it. In light of the Roman occupation of Palestine, it does not require much imagination to envision a Roman soldier pressing into service a Jew who is passing by. The same

2 *The Community Rule* at Qumran states: "A man who draws out his left hand to gesture during conversation is to suffer ten days' reduced rations" (1 QS 7). See *Dead Sea Scrolls*, 136.

3. Wink, *Engaging*, 179, views the man's nakedness as an act of protest against the wealthy and powerful, who controlled the society.

Greek verb is used in Matt 27:32 to report that Roman soldiers "compelled" Simon of Cyrene to carry Jesus' cross. Jewish Christians in Matthew's audience would well understand the resentment Jews would have experienced whenever occupying troops imposed subservience against their will. If a Jewish man was forced to carry a soldier's gear for a mile, his natural reaction would have been to grit his teeth and hate every step he was required to carry the onerous burden.

Jesus' instruction to go a second mile suggests an unanticipated action and calls for a shift in attitude for the person pressed into service. He must forgo his angry reaction in order to take the initiative and alter the power dynamics. His cheerfully going a second mile might cause the soldier to reflect on the practice of forced labor or embarrass him by calling into question his strength to carry his own equipment. Wink even sees intended humor in the described situation. He writes, "From a situation of servile impressment, the oppressed have suddenly seized the initiative . . . Imagine the situation of a Roman infantryman pleading with a Jew to give back his pack! The humor of this scene may have escaped us, but it could scarcely have been lost on Jesus' hearers, who must have been regaled at the prospect of thus discomfiting their oppressors."[4]

The final parallel lines about lending to the one who asks to borrow do not seem to fit with this series dealing with non-retaliation. However, Charles Talbert points to the Jewish commentary on the first part of Lev 19:18 which states: "But is it not written: Thou shalt not take vengeance nor bear any grudge (Lev 19:18). That refers to monetary affairs, for it has been taught: What is revenge and what is bearing a grudge? If one says to his fellow: Lend me your sickle, and he replied No, and tomorrow the second comes to the first and says: Lend me your axe! And he replies: I will not lend it to you, just as you would not lend me your sickle, that is revenge."[5]

In other words, Jesus is urging his followers to assist the needy neighbor and not to seek revenge even if that neighbor had previously refused to offer assistance. Such positive action would be enacting the rest of Lev 19:18 (". . . but you shall love your neighbor as yourself: I am the Lord"), treating the neighbor as you would want to be treated.

The four concrete illustrations in 5:39–42 do not present the Matthean community with an impossible ideal. Though radical, Jesus'

4. Ibid., 182.

5. Talbert, *Reading,* 90, is quoting *b. Yoma* 23a in the Mishnah.

directives are possible to do: turning the other cheek, handing over the additional garment, going the second mile, and continuing to assist the unlikable neighbor. Representing various arenas of Palestinian life, the examples demonstrate how the urge to retaliate pervades all areas of daily existence. Jesus is not simply interested in limiting revenge but seeking to address the *revenge mentality* so deeply rooted in the human psyche. His interpretation of "an eye for an eye and a tooth for a tooth" introduces a pattern of responses that imaginatively instructs his disciples to think and act differently. In the face of insult and injustice, they do not simply become passive victims but act in imaginative ways, without submitting to their impulses to seek revenge or resort to violence. Their alternative responses hold the potential of transforming the volatile situation. Although this way of responding does not guarantee a change in the person doing evil, it does entail that possibility and clearly offers the SM community a strategy for interrupting the vicious cycle of retaliation so prevalent in the first-century world.

KNOWING THE CULTURAL CONTEXT

The New Testament world was an *honor culture*, where for males everything was about protecting the honor of their name and kinship group. If, for example, a man were dishonored by a backhanded blow to the face, it would be imperative that he responded forcefully to this insult in order to defend his honor. As is known from more recent examples in history, the need to even the score can set loose a retaliatory cycle that becomes increasingly nasty and violent. If, as another example, a woman of one clan is sexually violated by a male of another clan, men from the woman's clan can swiftly exact revenge by killing the violator or one of his kinfolk. This in turn can prompt the first clan to retaliate with more killing, and the revenge dynamic is underway. In the ancient world and even in contemporary societies, once the vicious cycle of revenge is in full swing, it is very difficult to stop. The *lex talionis* attempted to control such outbreaks of violent revenge by setting limits. But Jesus saw that an even deeper transformation was needed.

Galilean peasants and many early Christians undoubtedly suffered frequent humiliations at the hands of the powerful in the imperial system symbolized locally by Roman legions. Jesus himself was treated with contempt and underwent one humiliating experience after another in the final week of his life. His crucifixion, imposed by Romans on criminals and slaves, not only entailed an excruciating way to die but also exposed him to public scorn and shame (Matt 27:39–44).

Typically people living under a harsh military occupation ache to resist and protest, but usually feel powerless and repress feelings of revenge. They sense no way to act in the face of the overwhelming force of the occupying powers. In first-century Palestine, Jewish revolts erupted sporadically against Roman occupation, with the most determined instance triggering an overwhelming and brutal response by Roman armies resulting in the slaughter of countless Jews and the destruction of Jerusalem in 70 CE.

Given the power of Rome, it is not surprising that most first-century Jewish peasants felt impotent to change their lot in life. It was within this environment of repression and brute force that Jesus calls for a non-violent, non-retaliatory manner of living. His followers were challenged by his words and actions to act differently, not merely defending honor but transforming violence.

ENGAGING THE TEXT TODAY

Many years ago, a professor of psychology participated in a class I was leading. As we discussed this passage regarding retaliation, he shared the results of a psychological study. The experiment was based on a sadistic game imposed on galley slaves in earlier centuries. First, ten volunteers were blindfolded and positioned in a circle. The psychologist gave one of the individuals in the circle a heavy switch and instructed that person to hit the person in front of him. Once this was done, the switch was passed on to the second person, who had just been struck by the switch. That person was then told to hit the third person as hard as he had been hit. In turn, that third party struck the fourth individual in front of him in the circle and passed on the switch with the same instruction. The key element was that each individual was instructed to strike the person in front of him *as hard as he had been struck with the switch* by the person behind.[6]

---

6. The psychology professor relating this experiment in social psychology was Dr. James Ulness, who recalls that this experiment was conducted by Dr. Philip G. Zimbardo of Stanford University.

As you might imagine, the psychologist had to halt the experiment before the switch got completely around the circle. The intensity of the striking had increased to a dangerous level. From that dynamic, the psychologist concluded that individuals' subjective perception of the severity of the blow inflicted on them is actually greater than its measurable intensity. When we humans are hurt and then strike out towards another person, we tend to increase the force of the blow. This psychological phenomenon explains why retaliation invariably escalates the violence. A similar dynamic operates between warring groups and even nations.

The human need for revenge is powerful and, some would argue, instinctual. When we are insulted or offended, we have an undeniable urge to get even or exact revenge. Athletic teams exploit such feelings to motivate athletes for defeating their opponents. Quarreling children show this proclivity to strike back and worsen the situation. Often adults' desire for payback can take more indirect and subtle forms, but it is nonetheless the potent motivation for their actions. It is not unusual for people to wait and plan for years to even the score with someone who snubbed or insulted them.

Against this background, Jesus' exhortation not to resist the one who does you evil (5:39) seems impractical, if not foolish. It is no wonder that most Christians do not take these words of Jesus all that seriously. Often his words have been understood as counseling passivity and submission. For example, sometimes pastors and priests have urged a woman living with an abusive husband "to turn the other cheek." Such use of this text is tragic and can even be criminal.

Jesus' way of responding to malicious acts of other people takes courage. Christians need not submit docilely to insults and abuse, but can act creatively and nonviolently to change the dynamics in such situation. This involves taking control of one's own response and recognizing one's own power to transform the situation and even the offender. Such action assumes the support and intervention of a community of people who trust the strength of the nonviolence Jesus advocates.

DWELLING IN THE TEXT

Quotes:

- "A black woman was walking on a South African street with her children, when a white man, passing, spat in her face. She stopped and said, 'Thank you, and now for the children.'"[7]

- "Wonder and surprise: *what if* you are a woman walking home from a supermarket on a deserted street, laden with heavy packages, and you realize that you are being followed? Here is what one woman did. As the footsteps behind her got closer, she wheeled suddenly, smiled at the stranger who was advancing on her, handed him her packages, and said, 'Thank God you showed up! I hate to walk alone in these streets, and these packages are so heavy.' He escorted her home safely."[8]

- "Evil will become powerless when it finds no opposing object, no resistance, but, instead, is willingly borne and suffered. Evil meets an opponent for which it is not a match. Of course, this happens only when the last remnant of resistance is removed, when the urge to retaliate evil for evil is completely renounced. Then evil cannot achieve its goal of creating more evil; it remains alone."[9]

Questions:

The starred questions are suggested for sessions less than an hour.

*What is Jesus here saying to his disciples?

*How can you "turn the other cheek" without becoming a victim?

In what ways do the concrete examples in 5:39–42 help us to know how to act?

*Describe situations in your own life to which this text speaks. What situations made you want to retaliate for something hurtful done to you?

---

7. Wink, *Engaging,* 191.

8. Wink, *Engaging,* 234–35, is citing this example taken from Dorothy Samuel's *Safe Passage on City Streets* (Nashville: Abingdon Press, 1975). See Wink, 390 n. 9.

9. Bonhoeffer, *Discipleship,* 133.

Why do we seem to experience this need to retaliate or get even with others?

*How do you feel when you seek revenge against someone?

*How do you feel when you refrain from taking revenge?

If Jesus' words are actually calling for imaginative, nonviolent responses to offences against us, how might his words apply to your life?

In what ways can your congregation take seriously these words of Jesus?

Why does this way of living allow people dignity and freedom?

*How does this way of nonviolent resistance accord with the gospel message?

Exercises:

1) Make available paper and drawing supplies. Invite participants to recall an intense situation in which they were deeply insulted or dishonored. After time to begin re-experiencing their feelings during the event, participants are to draw something that expresses those feelings. In the background agitated music could be played. Once sufficient time has elapsed (five or six minutes), encourage pairs to share and explain their "feeling-drawings."

2) Have the group members explore in pairs imaginative, nonviolent ways they might respond to another person's offensive behavior against them. Invite them to describe another's hurtful action and then discuss ways to respond consistent with Jesus' teaching in 5:38–42.

3) Select one or more of the quotes above and encourage the group to discuss the significance for them and their congregation.

Songs:

"Another Mile" (BC, 1:421)

"Bring Peace to Earth Again" (ELW, 700)

"When Pain of the World Surrounds Us" (ELW, 704)

"This is My Song" (ELW, 887; GTG, 340; TUMH, 437)—especially verse 3

"To Love Just Those Who Love You" (HFTG, 140)

"Help Me, Jesus" (TFBF, 224)

"Help Us Forgive, Forgiving Lord" (HFTG, 17)

Prayers:

O God, you are a God of compassion and justice and not of vengeance. Take our need for revenge and transform it into actions that create hope and peace in the name of Jesus, the crucified One. Amen.

Or you may use the prayer circle to close your session (see Appendix, page 159).

8

Blessed Community
—Open to Enemies

MATTHEW 5:43-48

5:43 *You have heard that it was said,*

"*You shall love your neighbor and hate your enemy.*"

5:44 *But I say to you,*

Love your enemies and pray for those who persecute you,

5:45 *so that you may be children of your Father in heaven;*

for he makes his sun to rise on the evil and on the good,

and sends rain on the righteous and on the unrighteous.

5:46 *For if you love those who love you,*

what reward do you have?

Do not even the tax collectors do the same?

5:47 *And if you greet only your brothers and sisters,*

what more are you doing than others?

Do not even the Gentiles do the same?

5:48 *Be perfect, therefore, as your heavenly Father is perfect.*

GETTING INTO THE TEXT

This important final antithesis exhibits a logical connection with the previous one: creative non-retaliation against an evildoer leads to doing good for the enemy. Some propose that the command to love your enemy is the most radical thing Jesus said, and in the Matthean sequence it provides a fitting climax, illustrating the greater righteousness to be lived out by the community of faith (5:20).

The first half of the command quoted by Jesus in 5:43 recalls a portion of Lev 19:18 ("but you shall love your neighbor as yourself"), a Scripture combined with the *Shema* of Deut 6:5 ("You shall love the Lord your God with all your heart, and with all your soul, and with all you mind") later in Matt 22:37–39.[1] The second half of 5:43 ("and hate your enemy") is not explicitly mentioned in Hebrew Scriptures but likely reflects popular attitudes and practice. In the biblical world, and in most cultures, defining your enemies is the flip side of knowing who your neighbors are.

Jesus' imperative in 5:44 uses the plural "you"—*all of you together* are to love your enemies and *all of you together* are to pray for the ones who persecute you—with the second parallel imperative explaining the first. Jesus can command the love of enemies because in his community love is understood in terms of action, not feeling. It is actually possible, though not easy, to pray for those mistreating the community. The four parallel commands in Luke 6:27–28 makes this point even more dramatically: Christians *can love their enemies by doing good to those who hate them, by blessing those who curse them, and by praying for those who abuse them.* Love is something more comprehensive than warm affection; it involves resolve and concrete benevolent deeds towards those disliked or even detested.

Matthew 5:45 offers the motivation to act in this radical way. The first portion, using the connective "so that," designates Jesus' followers *as children of God the heavenly Father* who act generously towards all people. As children of the divine Father, Christians are to practice God's ways in the world for God "makes his sun rise on the evil and on the good, and sends rain on the righteous and on the unrighteous." Thus, the motive for loving enemies is nothing else than the imitation of God.

1. See Mark 12:29–31 and Luke 10:27, as well as Gal 5:14, Rom 13:8–10, and Jas 2:8.

Interestingly 5:45b takes the form of reverse parallelism, by mentioning the recipients of God's impartial care in the following order: *evil ones . . . good ones . . . then righteous ones . . . unrighteous ones.* This literary device mirrors the hearers' tangible experience of reality. As people who strive to live according to God's "greater righteousness," they often are surrounded by those who act in evil and unrighteous ways. In the midst of such a hostile world, the SM community is instructed to love its enemies.

The next verses in 5:46–47 continue the argument for loving enemies by use of what in rhetoric is called a "contrary example"—illustrating *loving enemies* by contrast with what it is not. It in fact far exceeds conventional social morality of those who operate in self-interest or with malice. Jesus says that even the tax collectors act kindly towards those who repay them, and that even unbelievers greet those who greet them in return. In fact, greeting as a ritual of reciprocity was thought to involve a divine blessing and was practiced by everyone in the ancient world including Gentiles. Failure to return greetings would be viewed as a terrible insult and menacing threat to the slighted person. Exchanging favors and greetings represents how the Roman society operated, contributing to cordial relations, good business, and greasing the all-encompassing system of patronage. *Loving the enemy* is something far more than this.

"Be perfect, therefore, as your heavenly Father is perfect" (5:48) serves as the conclusion to this text—and probably to the entire set of antitheses in 5:21–47. The imitation of God motif that surfaced in 5:45 is here stated clearly and positively. Jesus' disciples discover the pattern for their character and practice in the nature and activity of God. The future tense verb in the first half of this verse (translated "Be," with a plural "you" implied in the verb form) can carry the force of a command or be understood as an eschatological future, indicating what they will become. There is no reason to choose between these two possibilities, since in this context it can function both as an invitation to behave in a certain way and as an end-time promise.

The Greek adjective *teleioi*, most often translated "perfect," is derived from the noun *telos* meaning "end" or "goal" and hence can signify "having attained the goal" or "being complete." In Matt 19:21, Jesus addresses the rich man: "If you want to be *teleios*, go sell your possessions and give to the poor, and you will have treasure in heaven, and come follow me." Most scholars suggest that the meaning of 5:48 implies a maturity or completeness in their all-encompassing loving—not moral perfection—for disciples patterning their lives after God's activity. This imitation of God extends even to the community's enemies, expressed in the parallel Luke 6:36 in terms of mercy: "Be merciful, just as your Father is merciful."

As already suggested, this final reinterpretation by Jesus serves as a climax to the series of six commandments addressed for the SM community. As the longest segments, the first and last are accented by their placement and seem connected. Nursing anger and grudges (5:21–26) puts people on the pathway of creating enemies. On the other hand, loving enemies (5:43–47) epitomizes a kingdom vision that seeks reconciliation at every turn.

KNOWING THE CULTURAL CONTEXT

The early members of the church lived in a violent world. They were, of course, keenly aware that their master Jesus, though he had posed no armed threat to the authorities, had been killed by Roman crucifixion, a most brutal form of capital punishment. Richard Horsley writes:

> The Romans not only conquered their subject peoples with massive use of violence, they also maintained the *pax Romana* by terror, i.e., by the threat and (when resisted) the use of further massive violence . . . Both during the conquest and periodically thereafter as necessary, the subject peoples were given vivid lessons in what the consequences would be of opposing Roman rule, such as the enslavement of 30,000 Jews in the district of Tarichaeae (southwest shore of Sea of Galilee) in 52 BCE . . . At times, even the slightest resistance such as a delay in payment of tribute became the occasion for brutal reprisal.[2]

It takes little to imagine how early believers in Jesus Christ would have been aware of the precariousness of their existence and would have normally avoided any behavior that would draw attention from those in control—Roman officials or soldiers, Jewish client rulers and their minions, or even wealthy landowners and temple leaders. In such an oppressive environment, it would be natural not only to fear those with power but also to learn to hate them.

There is, however, another dimension for people living under repressive conditions. Frequently, distrust and hostility surface among and

2. Horsley, *Jesus and Spiral*, 43.

between the people themselves. Under such daily pressure, people tend to vent frustrations in attacks against one another. They view other groups with suspicion. During Jesus' time, for example, Jews viewed Samaritans with distrust and enmity. Galilean Jews were considered suspiciously in Jerusalem. Within local villages, differences and disputes between people could be greatly magnified because of the pressurized atmosphere under Roman occupation. It is not difficult to imagine how kinship groups and entire villages could divide their world into *neighbors* and *enemies*, with the latter mistrusted, avoided, and even ostracized.

In Jesus' own teaching, the directive to "love your enemies" could well have alluded to the Jews' hatred of the Gentile occupiers as *enemies*, but its focus would surely have also been on *enemies* created among Jewish neighbors themselves (see again Lev 19:17–18). Animosities and divisions could have easily erupted in social and economic interactions of villagers who suffered food scarcity and other stress in their daily existence.[3]

If the Gospel of Matthew was addressing Christian house churches within the urban environment of Antioch, then the context for hearing these words of Jesus has changed by 75 to 85 CE. Imperial cities, like Antioch in the Roman world, would certainly have contained its share of diseases, poverty, and miserable living conditions for many residents, but the Gospel hints at an economically more secure status for many of its hearers.[4] Clearly there is evidence of the Matthean churches' contentious relationships with Jewish synagogue communities in Antioch (see 23:1ff.). But it is also likely that the Christians bumped up against imperial representatives as well as the ever-present Roman army. If 10:16–23 alludes to the Matthean context as well as the original Palestinian setting, then Christians in Antioch faced hardships and threats as they sought to embody God's reign in the world, an alternative vision to imperial domination. Creative nonviolence (5:38–42) and benevolent action towards even Roman enemies (5:43–47) were integral to Jesus' vision of that divine reign. By practicing them, the Christians mirrored God's merciful and transforming way within the world.

---

3. See ibid., 270–71.

4. For example, Jesus in Matt 5:3 states "Blessed are the poor *in spirit*" rather than "Blessed are you who are poor" (Luke 6:20), and Matthew's Gospel speaks of higher denominations of wealth than Mark when describing Jesus' commissioning the Twelve (cf. Matt 10:9 with Mark 6:8).

ENGAGING THE TEXT TODAY

Over twenty years ago I read Sam Keen's *Faces of the Enemy: Reflections of the Hostile Imagination*. Its core argument is that we human beings as *Homo hostilis* ". . . find excuses to hate and dehumanize each other, and we always justify ourselves with the most mature-sounding political rhetoric."[5] Stated more simply, although enemies can be real, they are often created by the hostile imagination of others. The book catalogues the various archetypal depictions of the enemy: as stranger, aggressor, faceless, barbarian, criminal, torturer, rapist, beast, and so on.

Over the last few decades, and particularly since 9/11, social psychologists have undertaken considerable research in what is termed *enmification* or enemy-making. This research has produced programs, including manuals to be used in workshops, designed to help people think about the psychological processes (e.g., stereotyping and dehumanization) that contribute to making enemies and how to moderate intergroup conflict and prejudice. One manual, first written by Stephen Dillon Fabick in 1986 and revised in 2004, is *Us & Them: Moderating Group Conflict.*[6] It includes visual materials and exercises that demonstrate how "Us & Them" thinking tends to exaggerate the goodness and exceptional quality of one's own group, while devaluing and fearing other groups.

Our deep impulses to divide the world into "us" and "them" undoubtedly have an evolutionary, biological basis—the need for survival and security. To simply surrender to this way of viewing reality, however, leads to brutal conflicts and deadly outcomes. Long before our current psychological awareness and research, Jesus' directive to love the enemy addressed the human proclivity to separate the world into "neighbors" and "enemies" with its damaging consequences—turmoil, discord, quarreling, fighting, violence, hate crimes, ethnic cleansing, warfare. His community of followers was not to be about enemy-making but peacemaking and reconciliation (5:9).

Loving enemies is the activity of the Christian community that most clearly separates its vision and practice from the surrounding society. Most groups in society reward friends and punish enemies, but this is not to be the way of Jesus' followers. The Christian practice of doing good to enemies, of blessing and praying for enemies, is not a slick strategy

5. Keen, *Faces,* 10.

6. Fabrick, *Us & Them* (based on a project of the Michigan Chapter of Psychologists for Social Responsibility, 2004) is available at www.psysr.org.

for changing enemies into friends. That transformation might occur, but Jesus does not guarantee it. Rather Jesus anchors this radical practice in the nature of God's action. By loving enemies, the Christian community makes known the very character of God, a witness that implicitly suggests that all people—in their great and sometimes frightening diversity—are created and loved by the Divine One and hence are our brothers and sisters.

DWELLING IN THE TEXT

Quotes:

- "I have decided to stick with love. Hate is too big a burden to bear."[7]

- "Love is the only force capable of transforming an enemy into friend."[8]

- "We don't see things as they are; we see things as we are."[9]

- To our most bitter opponents we say: "We shall match your capacity to inflict suffering by our capacity to endure suffering. We shall meet your physical force with soul force. Do to us what you will, and we shall continue to love you. We cannot in all good conscience obey your unjust laws, because noncooperation with evil is as much a moral obligation as is cooperation with good. Throw us in jail, and we shall still love you. Bomb our homes and threaten our children, and we shall still love you. Send your hooded perpetrators of violence into our communities at the midnight hour and beat us and leave us half dead, and we shall still love you. But be ye assured that we will wear you down by our capacity to suffer. One day we shall win freedom, but not only for ourselves. We shall so appeal to your heart and conscience that we shall win you in the process, and our victory will be a double victory."[10]

---

7. Martin Luther King Jr.

8. Ibid.

9. Anais Nin.

10. Martin Luther King Jr., "Love Your Enemies," a sermon written in jail for committing nonviolent civil disobedience during the bus boycott in Montgomery, Alabama, and delivered at the Dexter Avenue Baptist Church at Christmas, 1957.

Questions:

If the session is shorter than an hour, use the starred questions.

Focus on 5:43–45

> *What is Jesus saying in these verses?
>
> In Jesus' time, what people would Jews have considered enemies?
>
> *How would these words have impacted first-century Christian communities?

Focus on 5:46–48

> *How do you interpret these verses?
>
> How do you understand the word "perfect" in verse 48?
>
> How are you able to love your enemies? What are clues in the text (cf. also Luke 6:27)?

Concluding Discussion

> *Why is loving your enemy so outrageous?
>
> Why is it that we human beings tend to make enemies?
>
> Who are the ones you consider your enemies today?
>
> *What kind of world would we have if God did not cause the sun to shine and send rain on both the good and evil ones?
>
> *What does hating enemies do to them? To you?
>
> *How does loving your enemies change you? How might it change your enemies?
>
> How can your congregation take this passage seriously? When was the last time your congregation prayed for enemies?

Exercises:

1) This exercise involves the stereotyping of other people.[11] The facilitator prepares at least twenty cards with the name of group on each: Catholics, Lutherans, Presbyterians, Baptists, Methodists, Protestants, teenagers, old people, gays, Muslims, Jews, Arabs, blacks, whites, gun owners, pacifists, pro-life advocates, pro-choice advocates, Pentecostals, men, women, straights, welfare recipients, Asians, immigrants, Italians, Poles, Mexicans, rich, poor, conservatives, liberals, obese, labor, management, police, intellectuals, Northerners, Southerners. Have participants form triads and invite one person in each group to select one card, showing it to the other two group members. They in turn make disparaging and stereotypical remarks about the named group, while the cardholder refutes their comments and defends the group (two to three minutes). Then, as there is time, have the other two group members choose a prejudice-card and defend the group named. Finally, the facilitator invites the participants to discuss questions such as the following: *Was this exercise difficult to conduct? Why or why not? Were there common prejudices about the groups named? How did it feel when you were making prejudicial and stereotypical remarks? How did it feel when you were defending the stereotyped group? What did you learn about your own prejudicial perceptions and behavior?*

2) This exercise considers distinct groups in our society—black/white, Christian/Muslim, men/women, gay/straight, etc. Have the participants close their eyes and imagine themselves as a member of a group different from their own. Imagine how this other person proceeds through his or her day: waking up in the other person's home, going to the bathroom to take care of hygienic needs, looking in the mirror and seeing the new face, experiencing the body and dressing like the other person, taking on the customs and mannerisms of that person, leaving that person's house and proceeding to a public place of employment or schooling, seeing others and thinking how they are viewing you, what are others saying about you as you pass, later in the day attending a social gathering, greeting people and noting their responses, and so on. After about five minutes of this imaginary, visual experience, have the participants discuss questions such as: *How easy was it for you to visualize yourself as someone of another distinct group? How did this visualizing exercise make you feel? What did you learn from this exercise?*

11. See Fabrick, *Us & Them,* 87–89.

3) Discuss one or more of the above quotes.

Songs:

"God, When Human Bonds Are Broken" (ELW, 603; HFTG, 155; WOV, 155; W&R, 416)

"When Our Song Says Peace" (ELW, 709)

"Lord of All Nations, Grant Me Grace" (ELW, 716; LBW, 419)

"Goodness Is Stronger than Evil" (ELW, 721; GTG, 758; STF, 2219; TFWS, 2219; W&R, 296)

"In Christ There is No East or West" (ELW, 650; LBW, 359; TNCH, 394, 395; TUMH, 548; TH1982, 529)

"Where Charity and Love Prevail" (ELW, 642; GTG, 316; LBW, 126; TNCH, 396; TH1982, 606; TUMH, 549; W&R, 600, 603)

"When Will People Cease Their Fighting?" (TPH, 401; W&R, 622)

"When Love Is Found" (TNCH, 362; WOV, 749; W&R, 612)

"To Love Just Those Who Love You" (HFTG, 140)

"Make Me a Channel of Your Peace" (GTG, 757; W&R, 587)

"When the Poor Ones" (ELW, 725; W&R, 624)—especially verses 2 and 4

"Here Is Peace" (W&S, 3123)

Prayers:

Holy God of compassion, you invite us into your way of forgiveness and peace. Lead us to love our enemies, and transform our words and deeds to be like his through whom we pray, Jesus Christ, our Savior and Lord. Amen.[12]

You may wish to use a prayer circle to end your session (see Appendix, page 159).

---

12. *ELW,* 24.

9

Blessed Community
—Not Flaunting Religious Actions

MATTHEW 6:1–6, 16–18

6:1   *Beware of practicing your piety before others*

       in order to be seen by them;

   for then you have no reward from your Father in heaven.

6:2   *So whenever you give alms, do not sound a trumpet before you,*

       as the hypocrites do in the synagogues and in the streets,

          so that they may be praised by others.

   Truly I tell you, they have received their reward.

6:3   *But when you give alms, do not let your left hand know*

       what your right hand is doing,

6:4   *so that your alms may be done in secret;*

   and your Father who sees in secret will reward you.

6:5   *And whenever you pray, do not be like the hypocrites;*

       for they love to stand and pray

          in the synagogues and at the street corners,

          so that they may be seen by others.

> *Truly I tell you, they have received their reward.*

6:6 *But whenever you pray, go into your room and shut the door*
> *and pray to your Father who is in secret;*
> *and your Father who sees in secret will reward you.*

[The Lord's Prayer appears in 6:7–15][1]

6:16 *And whenever you fast, do not look dismal, like the hypocrites,*
> *for they disfigure their faces*
>> *so as to show others that they are fasting.*
> *Truly I tell you, they have received their reward.*

6:17 *But when you fast, put oil on your head and wash your face,*

6:18 *so that your fasting may be seen not by others*
>> *but by your Father who is in secret;*
> *and your Father who sees in secret will reward you.*

GETTING INTO THE TEXT

As a transition to the next major section of the SM, 6:1 cautions: *Pay attention to/be on guard regarding your righteousness/justice.*[2] The same Greek word *dikaiosynē* appears in this verse as is used in 5:20 introducing the section 5:21–48, but here it is usually translated "piety" because it focuses on three indispensable practices of Judaism: almsgiving, praying, and fasting. Jesus is warning against the danger of ostentatious piety—of doing religious acts before people to be seen and praised by them.

Close attention to the text reveals a repetitive pattern in 6:2–4, 6:5–6, and 6:16–18: an opening temporal clause ("whenever you . . ."), a disapproving reference to the behavior of hypocrites, a comment that the hypocrites are motivated by human recognition and praise, and a declaration that the hypocrites receive *only* human praise as reward for their

---

1. The Lord's Prayer is considered in chapter 10.

2. My own translation.

pious acts. Finally, and by contrast, the disciples' pious acts, done without public notice, are graciously recognized by God, who sees what is hidden.

This repetitive pattern is designed to produce a rhetorical effect on hearers. They hear common phrases not once or twice but three times, and are thereby summoned to take Jesus' warnings seriously and remember them more easily. These three "little satirical vignettes"[3] function like political cartoons. They poke fun at the hypocrites' self-aggrandizing activity in order to invite disciples into a different behavior—practicing these acts because of their intrinsic importance and not for self-serving reasons. This portrayal of the *hypocrites* (in the Greek "stage actors" or people "playing a role") would connect with Jesus' hearers because they would have undoubtedly observed overly pious persons calling attention to themselves through their almsgiving, praying, and fasting. Now the hearers must examine their own motives.

The first vignette in 6:2 caricatures almsgivers who employ a trumpeter to announce their good deed whenever they contribute to the poor in the synagogues and on narrow streets. These hypocrites, Jesus states, receive what they are seeking—human praise and recognition but nothing more. They do not receive God's approval for what they are doing. In complete contrast, Jesus exhorts his disciples to offer their aid to the poor in total secrecy (6:3–4). Although it is clearly impossible for a person to do something with the left hand without the other side of his body being aware, this exaggerated analogy captivates attention and registers its point. Religious hypocrisy is to be avoided by Jesus' followers at all costs. They are to practice their acts of mercy for the poor because they recognize almsgiving as following God's way.

In the second vignette (6:5), the hypocrites are satirized as ones who love to stand in the most visible public places for their prayers in order to be seen and praised by people (cf. also Mark 12:38–40). Jesus states that the only reward they receive is the human recognition they seek. Jesus' disciples, on the other hand, are to do their praying in a place where no one can observe them—the inner secret room in a first-century house.[4] Once again they have the promise that their heavenly Father sees and blesses their prayerful activity.

The final vignette in 6:16 comically pictures hypocrites distorting their faces to appear gloomy in order to attract attention to their fasting.

3. The phrase used by Betz, *Sermon*, 347. *Satire* is a social criticism that holds up to ridicule the foibles and shortcomings of others.

4. In 6:6, this is the meaning of the Greek word *tameion* (see *BDAG*, 988).

The verse with its play on two Greek words with similar sounds could be translated: "For they make their faces *unrecognizable* in order that they might be *recognized* by others as fasting."[5] Jesus draws the same conclusion: *They have their reward in full.* A contrasting manner for fasting is offered in 6:17–18: anointing the head and washing the face, the usual daily self-care, precisely to hide the act of fasting before other people. In other words, Jesus' disciples are to carry on in the normal manner so that only God notices their fasting.

Jesus' satirical depiction of the hypocrites draws a sharp contrast between two motives for practicing pious acts—a craving for adulation and approval from other people and a deep desire to do what is helpful to others and pleasing to God. Jesus' warnings alert his hearers to the corrupting influence of the human craving for attention and approval, a force that can co-opt even the most sacred endeavors. If those in the community of Jesus-followers do not scrutinize the motivation for their action, the community's witness can be severely compromised. Christians would appear like other groups as overly concerned to gain public praise and recognition, not as a contrast community functioning with a distinctively different motive—seeking to do the right deed for the right reason.[6]

KNOWING THE CULTURAL CONTEXT

Tobit, an apocryphal book written during the period 225–175 BCE, is one of numerous texts that suggest the prominence of daily prayer, regular almsgiving, and intentional fasting during Second Temple Judaism, the time of Jesus.

> It is good to conceal the secret of a king,
> but to acknowledge and reveal the works of God,
>   and with fitting honor to acknowledge him.
> Do good and evil will not overtake you.
> Prayer with fasting is good,
>   but better than both is almsgiving with righteousness.
> A little with righteousness is better than wealth with wrongdoing.
> It is better to give alms than to lay up gold.

5. My own translation.

6. These words echo the memorable line of Thomas Becket in T. S. Eliot's play *Murder in the Cathedral*—"The last temptation is the greatest treason: To do the right deed for the wrong reason."

> For almsgiving saves from death and purges away every sin.
> Those who give alms will enjoy a full life,
> but those who commit sin and do wrong are their own worst
> enemies (Tob 12:7–10).

For Jews to live righteously—in a manner responsive to God's expressed will in the Torah, it was essential for them to practice these three acts of piety. In 6:1–18, Jesus' teaching is not calling into question the importance of these three pillars of piety; rather he is unmasking the human penchant for perverting them into self-serving activities.

Additional information about almsgiving, prayer, and fasting can be valuable in appreciating the text under consideration. Almsgiving was seen as a benevolent activity characterizing a righteous person. To give alms to the poor was to do righteousness. The Greek word for almsgiving (*eleēmosynē*) literally implies doing a compassionate or merciful deed, exercising benevolent goodwill. Texts in Sirach[7] and Tobit suggest the following about almsgiving:

- This obligation, based on a divine commandment, invites liberal and ungrudging giving to the poor neighbor in need (see also Deut 15:7–11).

- Poverty was typically viewed as resulting from unfortunate circumstances, not God's displeasure, and could visit any Jew.

- Practicing almsgiving stores up treasures with God: "Lay up your treasure according to the commandments of the Most High, and it will profit you more than gold" (Sir 29:11). See also Sir 17:22 and 40:17.

- Almsgiving had the power to save from death and purge away every sin: "For almsgiving saves from death and purges away every sin. Those who give alms will enjoy a full life . . ." (Tob 12:9) and "Store up almsgiving in your treasury, and it will rescue you from every disaster;" (Sir 29:12). See also Sir 3:30 and 40:24.

Clearly almsgiving is fundamentally important as a merciful activity that supports the neighbor in need and pleases the compassionate God, who watches over the poor.

As demonstrated in Tob 12:7–10, prayer and almsgiving are sometimes juxtaposed as two interconnected acts (see also Sir 7:10: "Do not

---

7. Sirach was likely written before 180 BCE in Hebrew and later translated into Greek.

grow weary when you pray; do not neglect to give alms"). In later Judaism it was argued that almsgiving increased the efficacy of a person's prayer. Clearly prayer, as petition and praise, pervades the Hebrew Scriptures, most notably in the Psalms. By the time of Jesus, a regular rhythm of daily prayer was established—morning, noon, mid-afternoon, and evening. These hours for prayer could be practiced anywhere but certainly in the Jerusalem temple (see Acts 3:1). Through regular prayer, the righteous Jew demonstrated his dependency on God.

Fasting was also connected with prayer (see Neh 1:4; Ezra 8:21, 23). Fasting, the intentional refraining from food for religious reasons, becomes a most important activity in exilic Judaism. Yet it was only on the Day of Atonement (*Yom Kippur*) and during national calamites that fasting was obligatory for all Jews. Exceeding this expectation, men belonging to the group of the Pharisees fasted twice weekly (see Luke 18:12). Matt 9:14–17 reveals that the disciples of John the Baptist also fasted, a contrast to Jesus' disciples, who did not fast because his presence was understood as a time of celebration, not of mourning. Fasting was done in sackcloth with ashes on the forehead, chafing reminders of sin and signs of mourning. Only after Jesus' crucifixion and earthly absence did the earliest Christians engage in weekly fasting. *The Didache*, a Christian document of the second century, acknowledges the Matthean passage when it states: "Let your fasts not be with the hypocrites, for they fast on Mondays and Thursdays; but you fast on Wednesdays and Fridays."[8]

Even if the Matthean Christians did not practice weekly fasting, they would comprehend the purpose of Jesus' teaching in 6:1–18. His words, first spoken in a pre-Christian context where almsgiving, prayer, and fasting were mainstays of Jewish piety, draw attention to the danger of distorting religious acts. The Matthean community in the environs of Antioch existed in a Roman world where the wealthy and powerful elite lavished benefaction on a city by constructing fountains and public buildings. They did so to be acknowledged and lauded by the urban residents. In the midst of this ostentatious display of wealth, the Christians were to live quietly and without concern for public recognition.

---

8. My translation of *Didache* 8:1, 320–21.

ENGAGING THE TEXT TODAY

Jesus' words in 6:1–18 concern *why* people do important religious acts, what today we would describe as human motivation.

Some years ago Dan Olson, a teaching colleague, alerted me to the research on human motivation conducted by Edward Deci of the University of Rochester, New York.[9] Deci distinguished between *extrinsic* and *intrinsic motivation*. Extrinsic motivation means that a person in doing something is primarily motivated by an external factor. For example, a teenage boy learns to play the guitar because it is a way to become popular with the girls, not because he loves playing the guitar. Or a realtor attends church worship primarily because it will be helpful for her business. If a person is extrinsically motivated, the person does one thing to accomplish an unrelated goal.

Intrinsic motivation, on the other hand, implies that a person is primarily motivated by doing the thing itself, not for sake of its external benefit. Now the teenage boy learns to play the guitar because he loves music and enjoys playing. A person participates in Sunday worship because this activity holds meaning and value in itself.

Deci reports that he advertised and selected a few mothers with a four or five-year old child to participate in his research. Each mother came with her child to Deci's lab on three successive Wednesdays for thirty-minute sessions. Upon arrival, they entered the lab room where Deci was seated at a desk. Near the door by his desk, there were two chairs and across the room there was a box of toys in front of huge wall mirror. Deci invited the mother to sit down and then said to the child, "If you want to sit here and listen to your mother and me talk, you may. But if you think that you might get bored, you may go over there (pointing to the box) and play with the toys." Invariably the child chose to play with the toys.

The mirror on the wall by the toy box was a one-way mirror with Deci's research assistants stationed with stop watches and note pads on the other side of the mirror. Each assistant was to observe which toys fascinated a given child and to time how long the child played with a specific toy. The goal was to determine the child's favorite toy.

---

9. See, e.g., Deci, "Effects." When Deci included adults in his study, he concluded that verbal affirmation would increase a person's intrinsic motivation in doing a task while the reward of money tended to decrease that person's intrinsic motivation.

When the mother-child pairs returned the second week, Deci knew each child's favorite toy. To half of the children, he concluded his welcome the same way as he had the previous week: "If you think you'll get tired of listening, you may go to play with the toys." To the other half, he changed his directions. Knowing the favorite toy, Deci repeated the direction and then added, "If you will play with the red truck (the specific child's favorite toy), I will give you these bags of M & M's." Thus, for half of the children in the experiment, Deci was attempting to change the child's motivation for playing with the favorite toy. The child presumably would be thinking, "I'm playing with this toy because I am going to get a couple bags of M & M's." Half of the children now had extrinsic motivation for playing with their favorite toy. For the other half, there was no change.

During the final week, Deci and his assistants were seeking to discover which group of children would play with their favorite toys for the longest period of time—the ones intrinsically motivated or the ones who now had had an extrinsic motive to do so. Contrary to the tenets of behavioral psychology—which argues that behavior is largely a consequence of reinforcement and reward—Deci's group discovered that the children for whom the extrinsic factor of the M & M's had been introduced seemed far less interested in, even resistant to, playing with the "favorite" toy. By contrast, the children who were simply permitted to play with the toys they preferred continued happy engagement with their favorites.

This study led Deci to a number of interesting conclusions. Contrary to popular belief, extrinsic motivation will not keep a person enthusiastically engaged with a given activity. Further, he concluded that intrinsically motivated people will be able to persist in the face of obstacles, whereas extrinsically people (e.g., I play the guitar because I am seeking to attract the young women) are more likely to quit under discouraging circumstances. Jesus' words in 6:1–18 are addressed to his followers, who as a community face considerable pressure and distrust in the society. They could even face verbal abuse, slander, and various forms of persecution (see 5:10–12). For this reason, Jesus underscores this point: make sure that you are intrinsically motivated. Make sure that you are doing the right thing for the right reason. Focus on your acts of piety and worship for their own sake. Do not surrender to your strong desires for human approval and applause. Such matters are superficial and will not endure. Be about the work of God's kingdom for its own worth!

DWELLING IN THE TEXT

Quotes:

- "The last temptation is the greatest treason: To do the right deed for the wrong reason."[10]

- A story about St. Augustine: Augustine had a vision in which he met an elderly woman walking along a road. She was weighed down with a doubly heavy burden. Over one shoulder she carried a huge chain and over the other a bucket full of water. In his vision Augustine asked this woman: "Where are you going with your heavy burden?" She replied, "I'm going to chain shut the gates of heaven and douse the flames of hell, so that people who serve God can serve God for God's sake and for the sake of the service."[11]

- "Self-deception is the human phenomenon in which a person conceals the real story with a cover story that he or she really believes yet only half believes . . . Both Paul and Matthew see human beings as enmeshed in a self-deception that promotes a cover story of righteousness in order to conceal a real story of unrighteousness."[12]

Questions:

Here are questions for use with groups, the starred ones for shorter sessions. To ensure everyone's participation at critical points in the discussion, you may choose to utilize the process of mutual invitation (see Appendix, page 156).

*What problem is Jesus addressing in this text?

*Why were the practices of almsgiving, prayer, and fasting central to ancient Judaism? Should these practices be equally important to Christians? Why or why not?

---

10. The words of Thomas Becket, Archbishop of Canterbury, in T. S. Eliot's play *Murder in the Cathedral.*

11. Augustine (354–430 CE) was a bishop of Hippo in North Africa.

12. Via, *Self-Deception and Wholeness,* 77, 133. An important insight of Via's study is that in real life "hypocrites" are indeed "self-deceived" rather than viewing themselves as merely "pretending." See S. Taylor, *Illusions.*

*Why are we so prone to convert the most sacred acts into attempts to win approval of others?

Why does doing the right deed for the wrong reason distort the act?

How do you determine if you are becoming like the hypocrites?

*How powerful is applause in your life?

How does your desire for recognition affect your actions?

How much are pastors and other church leaders motivated by their desire to be popular among the people?

How can a Christian community foster acts of piety among its members without resorting to public recognition and rewards (e.g., names in the bulletin or plaque on the wall for gifts)?

How do Christians keep their radical fervor in the faith without becoming self-righteous?

*In what ways does our inordinate need to be recognized for "doing good" distract from a congregation's mission?

*How does our yearning for human approval and recognition relate to the gospel message?

Exercises:

1) Have participants mime the three vignettes of almsgiving, praying, and fasting as one person reads the passage. In the words of Walter Wink, "The value of mime is that, unlike role-playing, *each* person can identify with *all* the characters in turn."[13] Allow five minutes to prepare the mimes. Appropriate music could be played as the text is read and the mimes are undertaken. Then discuss what new insights were gained.

2) Invite the group participants to write a contemporary dialogue between themselves and people like the hypocrites portrayed in the three vignettes. In the dialogue, ask them why they act as they do, and then write down how they might respond. Keep the dialogue unfolding through several imagined responses (five to seven minutes). Conclude by discussing what the participants learned about the "hypocrites" and themselves by dong this activity.

3) Have the group choose one or more of the quotes to discuss.

---

13. Wink, *Transforming*, 117.

Songs:

"Deliver Us, O Lord of Truth" (HFTG, 41)

"Have Thine Own Way, Lord" (TUMH, 382)

"Jesus, Remember Me" (ELW, 616; GTG, 227; TUMH, 488; TPH, 599; W&R, 285)

"The Lord Now Sends Us Forth" (ELW, 538; GTG, 747)

"Again We Keep This Solemn Fast" (TNCH, 187)—focusing on fasting

Prayers:

O God of truthfulness, keep us honest about ourselves and others. Strip away all pious facades that are self-deceptive so that we can worship you truly and serve others genuinely. We humbly appeal to your mercy and forgiveness in Jesus Christ our Lord. Amen.

Other options include using a prayer circle (see Appendix, page 159) or the words of the hymn "Eternal Spirit of the Living Christ" (ELW, 402; LBW, 441; TH1982, 698; TNCH, 520; W&R, 475).

10

Blessed Community
—The Lord's Prayer as Model for Praying

MATTHEW 6:7-15

6:7 *When you are praying,*

do not heap up empty phrases as the Gentiles do;

for they think that they will be heard

because of their many words.

6:8 *Do not be like them,*

for your Father knows what you need before you ask him.

6:9 *Pray then in this way:*

Our Father in heaven,

hallowed be your name.

6:10 *Your kingdom come.*

Your will be done, on earth as it is in heaven.

6:11 *Give us this day our daily bread.*

6:12 *And forgive us our debts,*

as we also have forgiven our debtors.

6:13 *And do not bring us to the time of trial,*

> *but rescue us from the evil one.*
>
> 6:14 *For if you forgive others their trespasses,*
>
> *your heavenly Father will also forgive you;*
>
> 6:15 *but if you do not forgive others,*
>
> *neither will your Father forgive your trespasses.*

GETTING INTO THE TEXT

In the previous chapter, discussion of the Lord's Prayer was omitted even though it appears between Jesus' warnings about pretentious praying (6:5–6) and ostentatious fasting (6:16–18). Within the sequence of 6:1–18, this Jesus-Prayer provides a corrective to the self-promoting piety and mindless prayer described there. It redirects attention away from self to God's kingdom and the basics for human existence.

The actual prayer in 6:9b-13 is framed by two brief segments—6:7–8 and 6:14–15. Verse 7 offers a negative example of prayer: "When you are praying, do not heap up empty phrases as the Gentiles do; for they think that they will be heard because of their many words." The Greek word translated "heap up empty phrases" (*battalogein*) can also be rendered "to babble" or to "use many meaningless words," a sense confirmed by the word *polylogia* appearing in 6:7b, signifying "verbosity" or "many words." This criticism of pagan prayer as babbling repetitiveness likely relates to a magical notion of language. Betz states: "Since the words of prayer contain magical power—at least this is the assumption—repetition and multiplicity increase that power, compelling the gods to pay attention . . . that unless called upon in such compelling ways the gods do not care, and unless informed about the person's needs they do not know what to do."[1] Jesus, by contrast, claims in 6:8 that repetitive wordiness is unnecessary

---

1. Betz, *Sermon*, 367. He cites the Greek Magical Papyri that contain what he terms "seemingly meaningless magical gibberish." Though not gibberish, Acts 19:34 describes the followers of the goddess Artemis in Ephesus as incessantly shouting for about two hours the words "Great is Artemis of the Ephesians!" See also 1 Kgs 18:26–29, where the prophet Elijah mocks the ineffective prayers and actions of the prophets of Baal to get their god to respond. Probably in reaction to lavish and extended prayers in the Roman world, Emperor Marcus Aurelius recommends praying in "a simple and frank manner" (*Meditations* 5:7 as quoted in Talbert, *Reading*, 110). In Mark 12:40, Jesus criticizes the "long prayers" of the scribes.

since the omniscient God knows the petitioners' needs even before they ask.

"Pray then *in this way*" in 6:9a implies this communal prayer serves as a norm for all praying done by Jesus' followers. This is not simply a prayer to be repeated over and over; the Lord's Prayer is the model for all Christian prayers.

The prayer begins by addressing God as "Our Father in heaven" (6:9b). The vocative form of the Greek *ho patēr* for "the Father," some scholars argue, translates an Aramaic term *Abba* originally used by Jesus to signal a close and affectionate bond with God.[2] In this way, the disciples are invited to participate as beloved children in the personal relationship Jesus shared with God as a caring and loving parent. Even if an original use of *Abba* in the Lord's Prayer cannot be definitively established, the earliest church counted this Aramaic word worthy of preservation. It is paired with the Greek *ho patēr* in Jesus' Gethsemane prayer (Mark 14:36), and that pairing occurs twice in Paul's letters affirming Christians' identity as children of God because of their baptism into Christ (Gal 4:6 and Rom 8:15). Moreover, saying "*our* Father" links every praying believer with all others in the community of faith, and "in heaven" echoes a Jewish phrase that clarifies that the One being addressed is not just an earthly father. God is available as a loving parent and yet beyond human manipulation as the Holy One who acts on behalf of God's people and the entire creation.[3]

---

2. According to Jeremias, *Lord's Prayer,* 17–21, God was addressed as "Father" in the Jewish tradition (see, e.g., Ps 89:26; Isa 63:16; Isa 64:8; Sir 23:1,4; Sir 51:10; and Wis 14:3), yet the more intimate *Abba,* as a child addresses his father, was not used for God. More recent scholars observe that *Abba* was used more widely than simply by little children addressing their fathers and question Jeremias's original conclusion that *Abba* could be translated "Daddy" (see *ABD,* 1:7–8). Although Jeremias later acknowledged that this word was also used by grown-up sons, he still claimed that Jesus' *Abba* expresses a special relationship with God (*Prayers,* 62).

3. See Wright, *Lord and Prayer,* 14–15, who mentions Exod 4:22–23 as the first idea of "Father" since the passage speaks of Israel as God's "first-born son," a foundational notion as part of Israel's liberation from slavery. To quote Wright, 15: "The very first word of the Lord's Prayer, therefore . . . contains within it not just intimacy, but revolution. Not just familiarity; hope." Moreover, he connects this deliverance theme to that of the Davidic Messiah as "God's son" (see 2 Sam 7:14) and summarizes Jesus' message in the "Our Father" prayer to his followers: "You are the liberty-people. You are the Messianic people" (16).

Next, the Lord's Prayer includes three brief petitions that call on God to ensure the holiness of God's name, the arrival of God's rule, and the doing of God's will here on earth (6:9c-10).

Keenly aware of the otherness of God, post-exilic Jews substituted *name* for the sacred name itself—*Yahweh*. To speak of the holy *name* was to speak of God's availability and presence here on earth. The Jews were to honor the divine name (see Exod 20:7 and Lev 22:32), but frequently they did not, making it a laughing stock among the nations, according to the prophets. Ezekiel asserts that only divine action will be able *to sanctify the holy name*, accomplished by God's restoration of Israel to its land (see Ezek 36:19-24, especially verses 22b-23a: "It is not for your sake, O house of Israel, that I am about to act, but *for the sake of my holy name*, which you have profaned among the nations to which you came. *I will sanctify my great name . . .*") [italics mine]. This first petition in the Lord's Prayer similarly insists that *God* needs to act *to sanctify the holy name* on earth, what humans have failed to do.

The second petition in 6:10a reinforces the first one. God is called upon to bring the fullness of God's reign here on earth as the manifestation of divine love and justice that will sweep away all evil and injustice and be acknowledged by all peoples. This daring appeal for the full appearance of the kingdom of God here on earth implies the petitioners' involvement. They are pledging themselves to welcome this coming kingdom and be transformed by it, a reign of God they are already experiencing—though in a veiled way—in the ministry of Jesus Christ.

The third petition in 6:10b, lacking in Luke 11:2-4, builds on the previous one: the full arrival of God's rule results in obedience to God's will on earth so that peace and harmony will break out among people. The prayer's plea for God's kingdom to come and God's will to be accomplished on earth is tied to *the doing of justice* (see 6:33 that couples God's kingdom and justice). As in the opening beatitudes (5:3-6), these three "your" petitions invite the Jesus-community to focus on the coming of God's righteousness (Gr. *dikaiosynē*)—aspects of which have been concretely illustrated in 5:21-48 and 6:1-18. By praying the Lord's Prayer, the contrast community watches for and participates in divine action that brings transformation to them and the entire world.

The next three "our" petitions turn the focus to human needs here on earth, those of daily bread, forgiveness, and deliverance from evil (6:11-13).

The direct Greek translation of 6:11 is *Our bread for daily existence* [or *for tomorrow*] *give to us today*. *Our bread* in the emphatic first position suggests its importance. In that world, baked bread—something like pita or flat bread—was a basic staple in the diet. Yet, in this petition bread likely represents all foodstuff and other goods needed by humans for daily living. Marjorie Hewitt Suchocki points to the interdependence implied by the word *our* when she states: "To ask daily bread for ourselves is to ask daily bread for all, and to acknowledge our own responsibility in giving as well as receiving sustenance in this great chain."[4]

The second *our* petition, equally important to the survival of a community, centers on the forgiveness of debts: "And forgive us our debts, as we also have forgiven our debtors" (6:12). The Greek word used means "debts" (*ta opheilēmata*) whereas in Luke 11:4 a word best translated "sins" appears (*tas hamartias*). One scholar argues that "debts" and "debtors," as spoken by Jesus to Galilean hearers in 27 to 30 CE, urged debt-cancellation among peasants, who easily accumulated financial indebtedness.[5] Their plea for God's cancellation of their "debts" ("moral offences" or "trespasses" as in 6:14–15) was coupled with their willingness to release others from burdening debts, financial or otherwise.

Surely by the time the Lord's Prayer was included in Matthew's Gospel (75–85 CE), the terms "debts" and "debtors" were also understood figuratively, more like the forgiving of offenses against one another, a meaning explicit in the use of "sins" in Luke 11:4. Even so, the use of word "debts"—derived from the commercial sphere—suggests that sins are not simply a violation of legal or moral code but have to do with an "interconnected web of obligations" among human beings (and with God) that is often broken or damaged.[6] This petition stresses reciprocity between God's cancellation of our debts and our willingness to do the same for other persons indebted to us. This linkage between divine and human forgiveness was a notion widespread in Judaism in that time. Sirach 28:2–5, for example, states:

> Forgive your neighbor the wrong he has done,
> and then your sins will be pardoned when you pray.
> Does anyone harbor anger against another,
> and expect healing from the Lord?

4. Suchocki, *Presence*, 109.

5. See Horsley, *Jesus and Spiral*, 246–55.

6. Betz, *Sermon*, 402–3, develops this insight.

> If one has no mercy toward another like himself,
>> can he then seek pardon for his own sins?
> If a mere mortal harbors wrath,
>> who will make an atoning sacrifice for his sins?[7]

The final petition in 6:13 ("and do not bring us to the time of trial, but rescue us from the evil one") has been frequently interpreted as describing the severe tribulation at the end of history. It is worth noting, however, that the Greek word translated "trial" or "temptation" has no definite article and could also be rendered "*a* time of trial" rather than "*the* time of trial." This could signal a more general meaning of trial, not just the end-time testing. The Greek word translated "the evil one" in the NRSV can be rendered either "the evil" (in an impersonal sense) or "the evil one" referring to Satan. In either case, this petition emphasizes the reality of the threatening power of evil that confronts humans both in the present and final days. Only God can rescue us in these precarious situations of testing, a thought similar to what Paul claims in 1 Cor 10:13.[8]

The three-fold doxology ("for the kingdom, the power, and the glory are yours, now and forever. Amen"), which some Christians use to conclude the Lord's Prayer, was a liturgical ending added by the earliest church.[9] Similar to Jewish prayer,[10] early Christians must have decided that such a doxology was an appropriate way to conclude this great prayer bequeathed to the church by Jesus himself.

The final verses in 6:14–15 reinforce the unbreakable link between divine and human forgiveness. By using the plural "you," Jesus here warns the entire community, first with a positive form and then the negative:

7. *Sirach* or *Wisdom of ben-Sira* is a Jewish deuterocanonical/apocryphal writing dated in the second century BCE and is modeled on the Book of Proverbs. Also *Yoma* 8:9 in the Mishnah states, "For transgressions done between man and the Omnipresent, the Day of Atonement atones. For transgressions between man and man, the Day of Atonement atones, *only if the man will regain the good will of his friend*" (my italics).

8. 1 Cor 10:13 states: "No testing has overtaken you that is not common to everyone. God is faithful, and he will not let you be tested beyond your strength, but with the testing he will also provide the way out so that you may be able to endure it." See also Jas 1:12–15.

9. The doxological ending does not appear in the best manuscripts of the Greek New Testament.

10. 1 Chr 29:10b-11, e.g., includes the following words as part of David's prayer: "Blessed are you, O Lord, the God of our ancestor Israel, forever and ever. *Yours, O Lord, are the greatness, the power, the glory, the victory, and the majesty;* for all that is in the heavens and on the earth is yours; yours is the kingdom, O Lord, and you are exalted as head above all . . ." (italics mine).

"For if you forgive others their trespasses, your heavenly Father will also forgive you; but if you do not forgive others, neither will your Father forgive your trespasses."[11] The practice of human forgiveness gets positioned as the necessary requisite for the final appropriation of forgiveness (note the heavenly Father *will forgive*). The parable of the unmerciful servant in Matt 18:23–35 offers a narrative commentary on these verses. The community of faith needs to put into practice the amazing mercy of God, a notion already articulated in the Beatitude "Blessed are the merciful, for they will receive mercy" (5:7). The church-community needs to appreciate that mercy and forgiveness—like daily bread—are basic necessities for their life together.

KNOWING THE CULTURAL CONTEXT

Prayer is a universal part of religion, with participants of every religious tradition seeking to connect with and influence its deity or deities. Prayer was clearly central to Judaism as evidenced by the variety of prayers preserved in the Psalms (personal and communal laments, hymns of thanksgiving and praise, etc.) and throughout the Hebrew scriptures (e.g., Solomon's prayer in 1 Kgs 3:5–9 and Jeremiah's prayer in Jer 32:16–25).[12]

Jewish prayers differed from prayer practices in other religious cultures in the area of Palestine. According to James Charlesworth, Jewish prayers tended to avoid ". . . pleas for material possessions or rewards, or magical manipulations of a deity who could be controlled by special deeds or words."[13] For the biblical people, God is sovereign and compassionate, not One to be manipulated by prayers. God is the One who "hears" the supplications of the people. The psalmist declares, "I love the Lord, because he has heard my voice and my supplications. Because he inclined his ear to me, therefore I will call on him as long as I live" (Ps 116:1–2; cf. also Ps 4:3, 34:17, 69:33). God is portrayed as responsive to those who seek to live as God's people.

In the Gospels, the Jewish Jesus is portrayed as a person who prays regularly, sometimes alone (Mark 1:35/Luke 5:16; Mark 6:46/Matt 14:23;

---

11. In a quite different literary context, the positive form of this conditional statement occurs in Mark 11:25.

12. See Clements, *Spirit and Truth*, for the nearly one hundred prayer texts in the Hebrew Scriptures.

13. Charlesworth, "Prayer in Early Judaism," *ABD*, 5:449.

Luke 6:12). Luke, in particular, accents Jesus' praying at critical turning points in his ministry (e.g., Luke 3:21–22, 6:12–13, 9:18–20, and 9:28–29). In Luke 11:1–2, Jesus himself is praying just before his disciples make their request: "Lord, teach us to pray, just as John taught his disciples." Evidently John the Baptist had taught his followers a special prayer, just as Jesus now does.

Jesus' prayer for his disciples is obviously one that assumes community—it is addressed to *our* Father and appeals for *our* daily bread, forgiveness of *us* as *we* forgive *others,* and rescue of *us* from evil. People in biblical times, far more than most Americans today, deeply understood the *corporate* and *interdependent* nature of their daily existence. For example, the earliest Christians would pray "Give us this day our daily bread" with keen awareness of what *our daily bread* represented. Preparing bread for eating was communal, involving not only the final baking but also preparation of the soil, growing and harvesting grain, distributing the grain to markets, and the making of flour. All this assumes as well the gifts of God—fertile soil, sunshine and rain. *Our daily bread* would hence remind them of the multifaceted, rich collaborative process involved in securing the basic necessities for living as well as their connection with all who needed bread.

Another Greek word in that petition (*epiousios*) could mean "Our bread *that we need for existence* give us today" or "Our bread *for tomorrow* give us today." Either translation focuses on the *daily* needs for sustenance and assumes a social context in which people did not take for granted their next day's food.[14] Without modern technologies for irrigation and food preservation, biblical people knew all too well their constant dependency on the mercy of the weather and kindness of others for their daily bread. For them the concerns swirling around food were both *communal* and *daily.*

ENGAGING THE TEXT TODAY

To pray the Lord's Prayer is to pray across geography and time. Whenever we say the "Our Father," we are joining with Christians who have uttered this prayer for almost two thousand years and those who are reciting it today around the globe. This worldwide use of the Lord's Prayer is visibly

14. The rendition of this petition in Luke 11:3 states even more explicitly the *daily* need for food: "Our bread that we need give us *daily* (or *day by day*)" (my translation).

displayed in the Church of the Pater Noster on the Mount of Olives in Jerusalem. There visitors are surrounded by tiled panels of the Lord's Prayer in sixty-two languages,[15] a visible witness to the global communion of those who share the privilege of praying to our Father.

It is so easy for us to repeat the Lord's Prayer by rote, with little or no awareness of the revolutionary power of these words to reset our priorities. Church catechetical classes and worship formats have fostered the frequent recitation of the Lord's Prayer, which is commendable as long as pastoral leaders continue to remind people of the generous and radical impact of these words of Jesus. We do not have the right to pray this prayer; rather it is a generous privilege granted us by our Lord Jesus. As some liturgies state, it is only *with boldness that we dare to utter this Jesus-prayer.* Wright puts it this way: "When Jesus gave his disciples this prayer, he was giving them part of his own breath, his own life, his own prayer. The prayer is actually a distillation of his own sense of vocation, his own understanding of his Father's purposes. If we are truly to enter into it and make it own, it can only be if we first understand how he set about living the Kingdom himself."[16]

This Jesus-Prayer should become a lens for viewing Jesus' message and ministry in order to discern the implications for our faith community agenda. Praying and practicing the Lord's Prayer will shift our attention and energy to becoming *kingdom people* rather than narrowly existing as *church people.* It will focus our eyes on what God is up to in the midst of our community and beyond. It will direct our gaze to places of hunger and want, inviting generosity; places of anger and hostility, needing reconciliation; places of heightened strain and temptation, calling for protective care and intervention; places of crisis and disorder, requiring peace and perspective.

As an example of this bold understanding of the Lord's Prayer, a colleague Craig Nessan offered a surprising suggestion at a world assembly of Lutheran Christians. He challenged Christians voluntarily to place a moratorium on praying the petition "Give us this day our daily bread" until they begin to address seriously the scandal of world hunger. This suggestion was not intended as a clever gimmick but a wake-up call for

---

15. See Murphy-O'Connor, *Land,* 113–14.
16. Wright, *Lord and Prayer,* 2.

the church to be about eradicating world hunger that is both possible and ethically mandated by the Gospel.[17]

To pray the Lord's Prayer should prompt congregations to become increasingly communities of generosity and forgiveness, pioneering settlements on earth where God's reign of graciousness and justice are visible. Followers of Jesus do not recite his prayer as a substitute for action. Rather, praying the Lord's Prayer enables and shapes their action of sharing bread and forgiveness, even on occasions canceling the financial debts of others. Prayer and action must be theologically and practically interwoven in the life of a faith community. Ulrich Luz writes of this interdependence of prayer and action: "For Matthew, prayer is not a flight from practice but its innermost side. Prayer makes it possible for the disciples of Jesus to experience the demands of Jesus as the will of the Father and to draw strength from this. Prayer does not become superfluous by acting, but the acting remains constantly dependent on prayer."[18] In baptism we are given the Lord's Prayer as our prayer and at the Lord's Supper we are *bold* to pray "our Father." This *holy boldness* is to characterize our attitude and action.

DWELLING IN THE TEXT

Quotes:

- The "ourness" of the relation to father overturns the patriarchal privilege of "your" father against "mine." In a profound sense, the "our" in the petition radically reverses the societal exclusiveness of "father." When this reversal is recognized, a more authentic naming than father might be "our parent" . . .[19]

- Kingdom people seek first the Kingdom of God and its justice; church people often put church work above concerns of justice, mercy and truth. Church people think about how to get people into the church; Kingdom people think about how to get the church into the world.

---

17. Nessan has issued this challenge more fully in his book *Give Us This Day,* especially chapters 4 and 5.

18. Luz, *Matthew,* 389.

19. Suchocki, *Presence,* 106.

Church people worry that the world might change the church; Kingdom people work to see the church change the world.[20]

- It often appears that those who talk the most about going to heaven when you die talk the least about bringing heaven to earth right now, as Jesus taught us to pray: "Your will be done on earth as it is in heaven." At the same time, it often appears that those who talk the most about relieving suffering now talk the least about heaven when we die. Jesus teaches us to pursue the life of heaven now and also then, anticipating the day when earth and heaven are one.[21]

- How dare we come to the Lord's Table in a world where millions of Christian sisters and brothers lack daily bread? If we ask God in this petition for our own daily bread while we neglect the starving, it becomes tragically ironic that in the very next petition we beseech God for forgiveness. In our day, perhaps more than ever, these two petitions belong together.[22]

Questions:

For shorter sessions, the starred questions may be used.

*What prayers were you taught as a child? At what age did you learn the Lord's Prayer?

If God knows our needs before we ask, why is it still important for us to pray?

*What would it mean for your faith community to take the Lord's Prayer seriously as a benchmark for all your praying and action?

In what ways are our praying and acting interconnected?

Is praying "Our Father" problematic for you? Why or why not? (see the Suchocki quote above).

*Why are sharing bread and sharing forgiveness equally important to human community?

---

20. Bosch, *Mission*, 378, quoting Howard Snyder, who claims Christians should be called "kingdom people" rather than "church people."

21. Bell, *Love Wins*, 45–46.

22. Nessan, *Give*, 37.

*"My neighbor's material needs are my spiritual needs."[23] Do you agree with this statement? Why or why not?

What does it mean to pray for the necessities of life, not luxuries? How do we discern what is necessary for our living?

How are people facing times of testing today, from which only God can deliver?

Jesus' praying in Gethsemane discloses his struggle to do God's will (Matt 26:36–45). How do you struggle to pray and live God's will rather than your own?

*Why is this prayer of Jesus so important to you personally?

*In what ways does the Lord's Prayer bring us good news?

Exercises:

1) Assign one petition of the Lord's Prayer to the participants divided into six groups, inviting each group to compose a brief prayer for communal worship that reflects the meaning and concern of its petition (allow about ten minutes). If there is time, each group should read its prayer as part of the closing.

2) With the group divided into six units, each is given a 3" x 5" card with one of the six petitions of the Lord's Prayer written on it. After the subgroups prepare a mini-drama about their assigned petition, invite the groups to act out the Lord's Prayer in sequence as a fresh way of experiencing the prayer (ten to fifteen minutes).

Songs:

"Lord, Listen to Your Children Praying" (ELW, 752; GTG, 469; STF, 2193; TFBF, 247; TFWS, 2193; W&R, 489)

"The Lord's Prayer," (GTG, 464; STF, 2278; TFBF, 34; TFWS, 2278; TH1982, S 148, S, 149, S 150; TUMH, 270, 271; W&S, 3069, 3070)

"The Lord's Prayer" in Morning Prayer (ELW, p. 305)

"Our Father in Heaven" (TPH, 571, 589, 590)

"Forgive Our Sins As We Forgive" (ELW, 605; GTG, 444; LBW, 307; TH1982, 674; TPH, 347; TUMH, 390; W&R, 382)

---

23. This quote and follow-up questions appear in Nessan, *Give*, 38.

"This is My Song" (ELW, 887; GTG, 340; TNCH, 591; TUMH, 437)—
especially verse 3

"Golden Breaks the Dawn" (GTG, 668; TNCH, 470)

"Hear Our Prayer, God Above" (BC, 2:722)

Prayers:

You may use the prayers composed in exercise one, or you may invite participants to create a breath prayer using the Lord's Prayer. In the breath prayer, one inhales deeply and then says a phrase as one exhales: (Inhale) "Our Father in heaven" (inhale), "Holy be your name" (inhale), "Your reign come" (inhale), "Your will be done" (inhale), "on earth as in heaven" (inhale), "our bread for living" (inhale), "give us today" (inhale), "forgive us our debts" (inhale), "as we forgive those indebted to us" (inhale), "and do not bring us into a time of trial" (inhale), "but deliver us from evil" (inhale). "For the reign and the power and the glory are yours forever. Amen."

11

Blessed Community
—Replacing Worry with Trust

MATTHEW 6:24-34

6:24 *No one can serve two masters;*

> *for a slave will either hate the one and love the other,*
>
> *or be devoted to the one and despise the other.*

You cannot serve God and wealth.

6:25 *Therefore I tell you, do not worry about your life,*

> *what you will eat or what you will drink,*
>
> *or about your body,*
>
> *what you will wear.*

Is not life more than food, and the body more than clothing?

6:26 *Look at the birds of the air;*

> *they neither sow nor reap nor gather into barns,*
>
> *and yet your heavenly Father feeds them.*

Are you not of more value than they?

6:27 *And can any of you by worrying add a single hour*

> *to your span of life?*

6:28 *And why do you worry about clothing?*

Consider the lilies of the field, how they grow;

they neither toil nor spin,

6:29 *yet I tell you,*

even Solomon in all his glory was not clothed like one of these.

6:30 *But if God so clothes the grass of the field,*

which is alive today and tomorrow is thrown into the oven,

will he not much more clothe you—you of little faith?

6:31 *Therefore do not worry, saying,*

"What will we eat?"

or

"What will we drink?"

or

"What will we wear?"

6:32 *For it is the Gentiles who strive for all these things;*

and indeed your heavenly Father knows

that you need all these things.

6:33 *But strive first for the kingdom of God and his righteousness,*

and all these things will be given to you as well.

6:34 *So do not worry about tomorrow,*

for tomorrow will bring worries of its own.

Today's trouble is enough for today.

GETTING INTO THE TEXT

In the preceding sections, Jesus exhorts his hearers to give their hearts to "heavenly (not earthly) treasure"—that which has value with God (6:19–21)—and draws a sharp contrast between the person with a generous outlook (eye) on life and the one with the evil and greedy eye (6:22–23). Now in 6:24, Jesus declares that a person cannot serve both God and wealth, thus suggesting that material possessions and money can be elevated to the level of a god. This prepares for Jesus' words in 6:25

("therefore, I tell you, do not worry . . ."), forging a link between divided allegiance and anxiousness about one's security. Extreme worry about material things can be symptomatic of a basic loyalty issue.

The words of Jesus in 6:25–34 are rhetorically designed to attack the deep-seated problem of anxiety in human life. His first exhortation (*Do not continue to worry[1] about your life* . . .) assumes that his hearers are currently fretting about their daily existence. Given the fragility and uncertainty of life for ordinary people in the first-century world, anxiety over survival could haunt them. This justifiable worry is addressed by Jesus and refocused by some basic questions. The passage includes six rhetorical questions that serve to remind listeners of what they should already know. They are posed in a way to seek agreement. The first two follow the opening imperative in 6:25: *Life is more than food, is it not? And the body is more than clothing, is it not?* These simple, yet basic, questions imply that human existence cannot merely be reduced to "eating and drinking"—a proverbial phrase popular in the ancient world.[2]

Central to Jesus' rhetorical argument are two examples from nature. First, in 6:26, he directs his hearers' close attention[3] to the birds that are only casually observed during daily routines. More careful observation has something to teach about God's providential care. These birds seem to survive without engaging in the wearisome food-producing activities common to agrarian peasants. A caring God provides food for them. The follow-up rhetorical question pushes hearers to learn from watching the birds intently: *All of you are of more value than these birds, aren't you?* Provoked to answer "yes" to Jesus' question, they must reconsider their own feverish fretting about getting food and clothing. Implicit therein is a promise—God, named as "the heavenly Father,"[4] to whom they are to pray for their daily bread (6:11), will surely provide for them, who are far more valuable in God's sight than birds. Ordinary birds teach them this vital lesson.

1. The Greek prohibition employs a present imperative, indicating that *ongoing* anxiety is being addressed.

2. Betz, *Sermon*, 471–72, n. 283, lists examples of this notion in biblical and Hellenistic writers.

3. The Greek imperative verb has a prefix that heightens its meaning, changing it from simply "look" to "look intently" or "look directly at" in order to "give serious thought to something." See *emblepō* in *BDAG*, 321–22.

4. In the SM, references to God as "Father in heaven" or "heavenly Father" are frequent (5:16, 5:45, 5:48, 6:1, 6:9, 6:14, 6:26, 6:32, 7:11, and 7:21; see also "your Father" in 6:4, 6:6, 6:8, 6:15, and 6:18).

The second example from nature, offered in 6:28–30, is intended to magnify the effect of the first one. It comes on the heels of two more rhetorical questions, the first of which reinforces the futility of anxiety in extending our days (6:27). Beginning with another question ("And why do you worry about clothing?"), Jesus entreats his listeners to ponder anew[5] the wild flowers they see daily, which are brilliantly decked out even though they do not engage in the human activities of toiling and spinning needed to produce garments. The splendor of King Solomon, Israel's wealthiest ruler (1 Kgs 10:23, 2 Chr 9:22), did not match the splendor of these wild flowers. Jesus' ensuing question makes this historical comparison even more surprising since these gorgeous field flowers are described as dried-up grass that does not last and gets burned in the baking ovens: "But if God so clothes the grass of the field, which is alive today and tomorrow is thrown into the oven, will he not much more clothe you—you of little faith?" (6:30). Here again the reasoning moves *from the lesser to the greater*. If God lavishes such beauty on perishable flowers, God will surely provide necessary attire for human beings, who are far more valuable.

All this brings the hearers to the climax of the passage. Whereas Jesus' initial invitation not to worry in 6:25 captured their attention in the midst of their anxiousness, in 6:31 the recapitulation of this exhortation ("Therefore do not worry") functions more categorically. Now the listeners are challenged to take seriously Jesus' entreaty not to be overly anxious, in light of the examples of God's providential care. They are not to act like people who feverishly run about questioning "What shall we eat?" or "What shall we drink?" or "What shall we wear?" Such excessive worry is inappropriate for the followers of Jesus, who are to act differently from those unbelievers who do not trust a provident God (6:32). Believers are to give priority to God's agenda of justice and mercy, and in the process they will discover their needs met: "But strive first for the kingdom of God and [God's] righteousness, and all these things will be given to you as well" (6:33). This verse, according to one scholar, "encapsulates the theology of the SM."[6] Doing justice and righteousness (Gr. *dikaiosynē*) is how Christians participate in the coming rule of God already visible

---

5. Again, the prefix added to the Greek verb changes its meaning to a more aggressive learning and can be best translated "observe well" or "study carefully." See *katamanthanō* in BDAG, 522.

6. Betz, *Sermon*, 482.

in Jesus. The entire SM illustrates what *doing righteousness* actually looks like in concrete situations faced by a faith community.

With no parallel in Luke 12:31, the final verse in 6:34 is a maxim that concludes the passage with a common sense warning. It centers on the hearers' undue worry about the anticipated troubles of the next day. Jesus declares such anxiousness to be folly since there are more than enough *troubles* or *problems* in the current day to occupy a person's attention. As a follow-up to Jesus' priority exhortation in 6:33, this last verse asserts that seeking God's kingdom and justice happens in the messiness of each day's experiences. The kingdom comes in spite of the troubles and trials of every day. Excessive worry about physical needs can immobilize Christians and obscure their vision of God's larger purposes that are to give meaning to their living.

KNOWING THE CULTURAL CONTEXT

Life was indeed fragile and uncertain for first-century hearers of Jesus' words about anxiety. Contemporary scholars paint a fuller picture of what life would have looked like for village peasants living in first-century Galilee.[7]

First-century Roman Palestine's economy was based on agriculture. Most people lived in villages and worked the land in the surrounding area. Formerly peasants worked their own ancestral land and produced food for their own consumption. Villagers normally also performed the operations necessary to process the crops as well as make their own clothes.

By Roman times, this traditional self-contained way of life was threatened. Over time the elites (Roman officials, members of the Herodian dynasty, other powerful families, and wealthy priestly families) increased their land holdings in Palestine and exerted increasing control over the peasant farmers. These elite, living in cities, disdained manual labor and enjoyed a life of leisure and learning, yet their daily provisions (wheat, barley, grapes for wine, figs, olives, pomegranates, and honey) had to be supplied by the people of the countryside. With a standing army behind them, the ruling elite extracted an exorbitant percentage of what the land produced, typically 25 to 50 percent. They did so by

---

7. For this section I draw on Hanson and Oakman, *Palestine,* 93–121, and Stegemann and Stegemann, *Movement,* 7–52.

means of various taxes, tolls, and tributes. Even fishing in Galilee was controlled by the ruling elite so that most of the preserved fish went to the tables of the wealthy, while fishermen benefited little from their labor. In every aspect, ". . . the benefits in ancient economy flowed 'upward' to the advantage of the elites."[8] Although most people in Palestine dwelt in small villages on the countryside, it was cities that controlled both the urban and rural areas.

Daily subsistence for most Galilean families in Jesus' day was hence difficult and even precarious. Basic farming with the iron plough and animal power was laborious and time-consuming. The plowing, sowing, weeding by hand, and reaping with scythes were tiring. Compared to modern farming with tractors and fertilizers, crop yields were minimal— yields of ten to fifteen times the seed sown compared to over forty times today.[9] Although peasant farmers sought to hold on to their land tracts and keep their families self-sufficient, many peasant farmers were forced into indebtedness because of failed crops and excessive taxation. This sometimes resulted in a loss of land. Jesus' stories about tenant farmers and day laborers portray such tough circumstances (e.g., Mark 12:1–12 and Matt 20:1–16).

In light of the precariousness of their existence, it is not surprising that Jesus addresses the Galilean peasants' concerns about food and cloth- ing. By the time Matthew is repeating these words of Jesus, the context has changed with his hearers likely in the urban area of Antioch in Syria. Because the elites lived in the cities, their sumptuous lifestyles exploited other urban dwellers—artisans, merchants, custodians of public build- ings, domestic servants, and slaves. It has been estimated, for example, that Antioch with 150,000 inhabitants had a population density of ap- proximately two hundred persons per acre (compared to twenty to forty persons in most major U.S. cities).[10] This urban crowdedness—coupled with issues of sanitation, limited supply of clean water, infectious dis- eases, epidemics, famines, fires, earthquakes, and occasional riots—made existence anything but pleasant and safe for most urban dwellers. For this reason, listeners in Antioch also experienced apprehension about their daily existence and desperately needed to hear Jesus' message of God's providential care. As church-communities, they were to seek God's way

---

8. Hanson and Oakman, *Palestine,* 108.

9. Ibid., 98.

10. See Stark, "Antioch," 192.

of mercy and justice as an alternative reality to their own endangered state, an alternative reality expressed in their fellowship of supportive concern and its hopeful view of a future guaranteed by God.

ENGAGING THE TEXT TODAY

Dismissing someone's anxiety too quickly with a glib "O, just don't worry!" is bad therapy and bad theology. Jesus was not dismissive of his hearers' worry but took it most seriously. The anxiousness of marginalized people about the next day's meal and adequate apparel is quite understandable. Yet, Jesus' words do not address anxiety superficially but target humans' deeper sense of insecurity. Years ago, I read a book by Thomas Oden[11] in which he describes humans as always living in the present time with both a past and a future. He claims we often feel guilty about the past because we cannot change it, whereas we experience anxiety about the future because we cannot control it. Thus, *an unchangeable past leads to guilt*, while *an uncontrollable future produces anxiety*.

The experience of anxiety—and hence the need for Jesus' words— does not necessitate that a person today is living from hand to mouth. Well-fed Americans with freezers full of food and closets packed with clothing still feel anxious about tomorrow, particularly given the pervasive uncertainty about our futures today—of America, of the world, and even of the planet. Pressured by all sorts of challenges, we can become extremely edgy as we imagine an endless future against which we need protection and security.

In his book *Shantung Compound*, Langdon Gilkey came to this conclusion after experiencing life in an internment camp in China. The invading Japanese army compelled about two thousand people of various nationalities—business men, missionaries, teachers, and other expatriates—to exist together in a relatively small compound in Weihsien province during World War II. The people were comfortable enough to establish a small society together but close enough to the edge of survival that basic human tendencies manifested themselves.

Gilkey describes what happened when the camp received some 1550 parcels from the American Red Cross in January 1945, each one measuring three feet by one foot by one and one-half feet and containing foodstuffs that would last a person for four months. When the Japanese

11. See Oden, *Structure*.

captors decided that the 1450 residents in the camp—two hundred of them Americans—should each receive one parcel and with the Americans receiving an extra one, some U.S. citizens protested the decision. They argued it was not right to distribute in this way since all the parcels were legitimately American property and should be given only to the two hundred Americans. Then, in turn, each American with his or her seven-plus parcels could share with others as they chose. As you might suspect, this "legal" protest from a few Americans caused a stir and created major discord among the camp residents, delaying the proposed distribution. In light of the dispute, the Japanese finally decided to give just one parcel to every person in the camp, including the Americans, and then to return the extra parcels to the Red Cross.

Reflecting on this unhappy situation, Gilkey writes: "Only the human mind could look far into the future and see that four or five large parcels would run out over several months' time; then, noting that distant peril, decide that at least seven would be needed for its security. A merely instinctive or animal reaction would have required only a momentary satisfaction. It is above all our frightened human spirits that, when we become fully aware of present and future perils, move quickly to protect themselves against all the contingencies of life."[12]

Jesus, in this text, is speaking to "our frightened human spirits" with awareness "of present and future perils." Today we could list numerous possibilities—analyzed incessantly by the media—that are looming threats to us: joblessness, domestic and public violence, volatile financial markets, menacing storms, threatening attacks, gridlock in politics, shifting political landscape in the Middle East, financial fault lines in the European Union. It would be easy enough to allow fear of the future to envelope us, and the contingencies of the daily news to toss us about like a boat without a rudder.

For us, too, Jesus' words in 6:25–34 provide a lifeline. They remind us that we have a caring God who provides for all creatures, even lowly birds and flowers in the fields, and that God cares for us as those lovingly valued far beyond these birds and flowers. In Jesus, we have been granted immeasurable worth as children of God and have been invited to join his mission of practicing mercy and justice in this world. In light of this identity and mission, excessive anxiousness on our part is inappropriate and only immobilizes us, causing us to lose sight of God's rich promises

12. Gilkey, *Compound*, 114.

for our living. It can even distort how we see ourselves—as less than precious children of God. Whenever we become beset and buffeted about by our anxieties, Jesus' priority-setting exhortation in 6:33 calls us to refocus our vision by attending to God's justice and his kingdom. Then most of our basic needs are met.

DWELLING IN THE TEXT

Quotes:

- But little Mouse, you are not alone,
  In proving foresight may be vain:
  The best laid schemes of mice and men
  Go often awry,
  And leave us nothing but grief and pain,
  For promised joy!
  Still you are blest, compared with me!
  The present only touches you:
  But oh! I backward cast my eye,
  On prospects dreary!
  And forward, though I cannot see,
  I guess and fear![13]

- "It is when we all play safe that we create a world of utmost insecurity."[14]

- "It is tough to make predictions, especially about the future."[15]

Questions:

For sessions shorter than one hour, use the starred questions.

---

13. Standard English translation of Robert Burns's words in his poem "To a Mouse: On Turning Her Up in Her Nest with the Plough." See "To a Mouse" on Wikipedia.

14. Words of Dag Hammarskjold.

15. A saying of Yogi Berra.

Focus on 6:24–25

> *What is the connection between the content of 6:24 and 6:25–34, as shown by the "therefore" in 6:25?

> Are there signs that our American society is serving wealth more than God (see 6:24)? If so, what are these signs?

> *Do you worry? Why?

> If we have enough to meet our physical needs, why can we still be so anxious?

Focus on 6:26–33

> *What are hearers to learn about themselves by means of Jesus' two examples of the birds and wild flowers?

> How would you describe the distinction between "anxiously striving for" and knowing that you "need" material goods for living (as noted in 6:32)?

> *What's involved in "seeking first" God's kingdom (reign) and righteousness?

> How does kingdom-seeking eliminate excessive worrying in our lives?

> *How does one live in the present, not the past or the future (see 6:34)?

> *What is happening today to make people very anxious about their futures?

Concluding Questions

> When you experience excessive anxiousness about the future, how does your life get out of balance?

> *How is anxiety related to our sense of identity and purpose in life?

> In your own words, what is the message of this passage for you?

Exercises:

1) After supplying paper and pencils, invite participants to find a quiet place to think and write. Each should complete the following statement with at least three or four words or phrases: *For a meaningful life in this*

world, I need . . . (use five minutes for completing the exercise and five minutes for sharing what was written).

2) Share a brief recorded segment of a current TV sitcom depicting characters with an affluent lifestyle, whose conversation and activity seem shallow and without deep purpose. Follow with pairs discussing the following question: *After viewing this clip, what about Jesus' words in 6:24–34 strikes you more forcefully?* If there is time, invite the pairs to share their new insights with the group.

3) The facilitator may choose to conclude the session with a guided meditation on the passage.[16] Invite the participants to assume a comfortable position, quiet their minds, close their eyes, and be ready to imagine, breathing deeply and slowly. The facilitator will read 6:24–25, pausing between phrases, and then say softly: *Think about the masters in your life. What things do you worry about? What concerns you? What does worry feel like for you? Pay attention to your body. What does it tell you? Are you feeling anxious?*

Next the facilitator reads 6:26–27 and elaborates: *Imagine the birds around you as you walk through an open area. Then watch them take flight. Leave your worries as you follow them into the air. Breathe slowly and deeply as you glide with the birds. Remain a moment in that scene.*

Next the leader reads 6:28–31 and continues: *Breathe slowly and imagine yourself in a spring field with blooming wild flowers. What does it feel like? What is your body telling you? Stay a moment in that place. Jesus reminds us, ". . . indeed your heavenly Father knows that you need all these things." What does it mean to you that God knows all your needs? Let go and trust. Imagine your worries fading as you hear Jesus' words. Breathe slowly and deeply. Remain in this restful place for a moment.*

Finally, the facilitator invites the participants gradually to return from their meditative journey as the concluding verses of the text are read (6:33–34).

Songs:

"Seek Ye First the Kingdom of God" (GTG, 175; WOV, 783; TFBF, 149; TUMH, 405; TPH, 333; TH1982, 711; W&R, 349)

"Seek for the Kingdom with All of Your Powers!" (HFTG, 36)

16. This guided meditation on Matt 6:24–34 was led in a Wartburg Seminary class by Jackie Cook.

"Great Are Your Mercies, O My Maker" (TPH, 352)

"What Shall We Eat?" (BC, 2:552)

"His Eye Is On the Sparrow" (STF, 2146; TFBF, 252; TFWS, 2146)

"Children of the Heavenly Father" (ELW, 781; TUMH, 141; W&R, 83)

"All Depends on Our Possessing" (ELW, 589)

"God Will Take Care of You" (TFBF, 200; TUMH, 130)

"Great Is Thy Faithfulness" (ELW, 733; GTG, 39; TFBF, 283; TNCH, 423; TPH, 276; TUMH, 140; WOV, 771; W&R, 72; W&S, 3106)

Prayers:

Compassionate God, you are like a parent caring for us. Sustain us in days of scarcity and disturb us in days of plenty. Keep our eyes and hearts fixed on your transforming work around us, giving us time for sharing love and seeking justice with little space for fretting and worrying. We pray in responsiveness to your gracious word shown in Jesus Christ. Amen.

You may wish to use a prayer circle to end your session (see Appendix, page 159).

12

Blessed Community —Freed from Playing Judge

MATTHEW 7:1-5

> 7:1 *Do not judge, so that you may not be judged.*
>
> 7:2   *For with the judgment you make you will be judged,*
>   *and the measure you give will be the measure you get.*
>
> 7:3 *Why do you see the speck in your neighbor's eye,*
>   *but do not notice the log in your own eye?*
>
> 7:4 *Or how can you say to your neighbor,*
>   *"Let me take the speck out of your eye,"*
>   *while the log is in your own eye?*
>
> 7:5 *You hypocrite,*
>   *first take the log out of your eye,*
>   *and then you will see clearly*
>   *to take the speck out of your neighbor's eye.*

GETTING INTO THE TEXT

With this text Jesus warns his followers against judging one another. Though quite brief, this text on judging is carefully crafted and rhetorically convincing. It can be outlined quite simply: an opening prohibition against judging (7:1), the reason for avoiding the judging game (7:2), exaggerations in the form of two rhetorical questions (7:3–4), and a final exhortation addressed to the hypocrite who presumes to pass judgment on a brother or sister in the community (7:5).

The opening prohibition against judging employs a negative in the Greek together with a present tense imperative of the verb *krinō*, indicating a ban on activity in which the hearers continually engage. Using the plural "you" Jesus thus begins by warning the entire community, "Do not *continue to judge*, so that you may not be judged" (my alteration of the NRSV translation). All are to cease what they often gleefully undertake—criticizing or finding fault with others. The parallel verse in Luke 6:37 ("Do not judge, and you will not be judged; *do not condemn, and you will not be condemned*") confirms this interpretation by clarifying Jesus' initial prohibition with the second warning "do not condemn."

The second portion of the 7:1 ("so that you may not be judged") is structured as a purpose clause and employs a passive voice verb. The passive voice implies that the hearers, if they keep on passing judgment on others, will be judged *by someone*. This could refer to future judgment by God, but the ambiguity of the passive voice leaves open other possibilities. Jesus could be saying: *If you continue to be judgmental towards others, then judgment will come back like a boomerang to you from others and eventually from God*. One New Testament commentator puts it, "The habit of passing judgment on others also involves a mechanism of tit for tat. The kind of judgment one passes on others comes back to the person who started it. Gossipers become targets of gossip; critics must face being criticized, and so forth."[1] In a negative way, this anticipates the Golden Rule introduced by Jesus in 7:12 ("In everything do to others as you would have them do to you").

7:2 provides the reason for the initial prohibition by advancing a clear connection between *judging* and *being judged* ("For with the judgment you make you will be judged, and the measure you give will be the measure you get"). This *measure for measure* principle, drawn from the market domain of measuring out grain, reflects how the world operates.

1. Betz, *Sermon*, 490.

The parallel sayings in 7:2 each end with a future passive voice verb ("you will be judged and . . . will be measured out to you"), suggesting both future "tit for tat" transactions among humans and God's end-time reckoning.

This text is so striking and memorable because of the exaggeration introduced by Jesus in 7:3–5. As previously (6:2–4, 6:5–6, and 6:16–18), Jesus uses hyperbole with great effect. Like a cartoon, the figure of the person is comic since he is attempting to get at the speck[2] in his neighbor's eye while simultaneously having a huge log or plank[3] protruding from his own eye. The scene is laughable since hearers easily recognize that this judgmental person is in no position to extract the speck. He could not even get near to the other person!

The two rhetorical questions in 7:3–4 are designed to help the audience grasp the utter seriousness of this rather humorous example. Both questions utilize the singular "you" in Greek to challenge each person in the community to consider the grave implications of Jesus' warning. The follow-up question in 7:4 rhetorically reinforces the first one in 7:3. The "fault-finding" mission of the critic is exposed: *"Or how can you say to your brother or sister, 'Let me take the speck out of your eye,' yet behold the plank in your eye?"*[4] In the second question, the Greek word for "behold" communicates a note of surprise. The person bent on condemning others is in fact incapable of isolating the small speck due to the huge plank blocking his own vision.

Jesus concludes his clever word-picture by addressing the would-be judge "You *hypocrite* (in Gr., "play-actor" or "pretender"),[5] first take the log out of your own eye, and then you will see clearly to take the speck out of your neighbor's eye" (7:5). By addressing the critic as hypocrite, Jesus suggests that the person is playing a role—that of judge—that is not legitimately his to exercise. Only God is in the position to judge human beings. The exaggerated difference between *speck* and *log* makes it unthinkable that hearers could ever imagine themselves qualified to play

2. *BDAG*, 510–11, offers the following meanings for the Greek word *karphos*: "a small piece of straw, chaff, or wood, to denote something quite insignificant, *speck, splinter, chip.*"

3. *BDAG*, 256, has the following meanings for the Greek word *dokos*: "a piece of heavy timber such as a beam used in roof construction or to bar a door, *beam of wood.*"

4. My own translation.

5. *BDAG*, 1038.

judge over another "brother" or "sister"[6] in the faith community. Tackling this insidious appetite on the part of humans to criticize and put down others is exceedingly important, lest the faith-community be divided or even destroyed from within.

KNOWING THE CULTURAL CONTEXT

The Matthean house churches hearing these warnings resided in a Roman society extremely conscious of class and status. Clear distinctions existed between the ruling class (the few) and those ruled (the many), men and women, free men and slaves, and even between freeborn and freedmen. Freedmen were former slaves who had been granted or had obtained their freedom. If ex-slaves presumed precedence over Romans of a good family, they were indignantly put in their "place" by those of higher station. Ramsay MacMullen states: ". . . it was the duty of every citizen to preserve [class] not only by his own fitting behavior but a prompt rebuke to anyone that tried to rise too high. 'Rank must be preserved,' said Cicero."[7]

In the Roman world, social stratification and rank were especially enforced by the ruling class—through titles, clothing, education, public speeches, seating arrangements at public events, place and size of dwellings, quality of food served at dinner gatherings, and even by verbal disdain and ridicule targeting the lowly on the streets. In such a class-conscious environment it is not difficult to imagine how those of higher rank could deliberately pass judgment on and dismiss others around them.

Although in first-century Palestine a ruling elite existed among the Jewish population (the Herodian family and priestly leaders), a deeper theme of equality before God was embedded within the scriptural tradition. Fair and kind treatment of a fellow Israelite, no matter the social status, was expected and guaranteed by God. And those who mistreated or demeaned others should expect similar behavior to return to them. This *measure for measure* principle, articulated in the text, is explicitly described in the Mishnah, the written compilation and categorization of

---

6. The three-fold use of the Greek word *adelphos* (brother) in 7:3–5 indicates that Jesus is addressing the judgmental tendency directed at other members of the faith-community. The NRSV employs "neighbor" that tends to broaden the term's application, perhaps helpfully.

7. MacMullen, *Relations*, 105.

Jewish law: "By that same measure by which a man metes out [to others], they mete out to him."[8]

Hence, Jesus' words in 7:1–5 address a demeaning activity all too prevalent in first-century Roman world—one person dismissing others deemed socially inferior or subordinate. Jesus bans this condemnatory activity because it calls into question the God-bestowed dignity and worth of other human beings and fractures community.

ENGAGING THE TEXT TODAY

With self-awareness, we recognize our penchant to view ourselves more favorably than we do others. If we were to create that entertaining scene of the speck and log used in 7:3–5, for example, we would have likely reversed the image. Our version of the word-picture might be: "I realize that I am not perfect, that I have *a speck* in my eye, *but* look at that other guy and his problem, *a log* in his eye." Our tendency is to minimize our own failing and magnify the offense of the other person. It is as though we are wired to think well of ourselves, while putting the worst construction on the behavior of our neighbor—quite contrary to Martin Luther's explanation of the eighth commandment.[9]

In recent years, studies in social psychology confirm these human proclivities. Certain studies have focused on our tendency *to find fault* with others' behavior,[10] while other studies have examined our propensity to justify questionable decisions and harmful acts that we do.[11] Taken together, these studies expose how we humans tend to function—blaming and criticizing others while giving ourselves the benefit of the doubt.

G. H. Morris's analysis of numerous transcripts of "fault-finding" situations was designed to discover the multiple methods used to register dissatisfaction with the behavior of another person. Focused on past events, "fault-finders" perceive a problem in another's behavior and call attention to it by a direct or indirect accusation, even demanding an explanation. The offender is *reproached* and must offer some defense of

---

8. As translated by Jacob Neusner in the Mishnah, *Sota* 1:7.

9. Luther's explanation reads in part, "Instead we are to come to their defense, speak well of them, and interpret everything they do in the best possible light." See Kolb and Wengert, eds., *Book,* 353.

10. See Morris, "Finding Fault," 1–25.

11. See Tavris and Aronson, *Mistakes.*

what he or she has done or said. The criticizing person can also focus on a present situation and challenge another person to stop a certain activity, often demanding that person to explain why they were doing it. Finally, even warning another person about future possible wrong actions can be a way of casting blame.

This sophisticated analysis by Morris demonstrates the manifold methods human beings employ to monitor and judge the behavior of others. In particular relationships—such as parent and child, teacher and student, or employer and employee—the ability to evaluate the performance and thinking of others is necessary and good. Yet Jesus' words in 7:1–5 are not challenging our *evaluating* others but rather our *judging* others. This *judging* seems rooted in our propensity to *find fault* with others who do not conform to social expectations or our own standards.

Our tendency to excuse or explain away any decision or action on our part, which we sense is in tension with our overall self-perception, contributes to personal blindness about ourselves.[12] Yet, so often, this failure in self-awareness seems not to check our eagerness to play judge over other people's beliefs, decisions, and behavior. This is indeed a dangerous game. If we take up the role of judge too often, we can become *judgmental* persons who are constantly finding fault with others and disdaining any who do not meet our expectations. Such *judgmentalism* can take hold of a person and sadly reveal a person who views all of life as "under judgment." Other people are potential judges of them, and God is viewed primarily as "the Judge."

When this kind of judging becomes widespread in a community, that community is at risk. Judgmentalism, which has the power to destroy families and devastate congregations, has no place in the Christian community. This does not mean that there is no room for a ministry of admonition and correction aimed at members who sin and engage in unhealthy behavior (see Matt 18:15–20), but Jesus' arresting word-picture of the speck and log outlaws all attempts to pass judgment on others. Because our judgments of others are so flawed and partial, they do not enhance relationships in a community but tend to undermine them. Refraining from *fault-finding* and *passing judgment* becomes an expression of the good news that all persons are loved and treasured by God. This contributes to making the congregation a hospitable place where nobody

12. Tarvis and Aronson provide numerous examples of how individuals will typically justify themselves even when presented with abundant evidence that their decision was wrong and their action harmful.

is placed under judgment. Life-together can thrive and offer an environment quite different from the surrounding society. Community members can enjoy the latitude to work together for the sake of the kingdom, open to one another's counsel and correction but free from harmful criticism and condemnation.

DWELLING IN THE TEXT

Quotes:

- The story goes that a man wishing to find a place to settle drove into a rural community and inquired of an old farmer what kind of people lived there. In reply, the farmer asked, "Stranger, what kind of people live in the community you came from?" "They are bad people," he said. "Gossips, slanderers, cheapskates." The old man shook his head, "You might as well move on," he said, "because that's the kind of people who live here, too."

  Later on, another man came through seeking a place to live, and he asked the same old farmer about the people. "How were the people where you came from?" inquired the farmer. "Wonderful, simply wonderful," he said. "They were thoughtful, kind, loving. I surely hated to leave them." "Unload," beamed the farmer, "because that's the kind of people you'll find around here."[13]

- "It is hard to see the beam in our own eye, but others can see it for us."[14]

- "We judge ourselves by our ideals, others by their action."[15]

- "Someone said of H. Richard Niebuhr (one of the most important Christian thinker of the twentieth century) that at one time or another he doubted every Christian doctrine except the doctrine of original sin."[16]

13. This story is included in the chapter on Matt 7:1–5 in Jordan, *Sermon*, 102–3.

14. Spoken by Emily Townes in her lecture at Wartburg Seminary, Dubuque, Iowa, in March 2003.

15. Spoken by Joe Volk in his presentation at Clarke University, Dubuque, Iowa, in April 2002.

16. This anecdote was told me by my former colleague at Concordia College (Moorhead, MN), James L. Haney, who earned his doctorate in Religious Studies at

- "All judging presupposes the most dangerous self-deception, namely, that the word of God applies differently to me than it does to my neighbor. I claim an exceptional right in that I say: forgiveness applies to me, but condemnation applies to the other person."[17]

Questions for Discussion:

If the Bible study session is less than an hour, it is best to use only the starred questions. The mutual invitation process may be utilized when appropriate (see Appendix, page 156).

Focus on 7:1–2

> *What is Jesus warning us about in this text?
>
> *What is the difference between evaluating another person and judging that person?
>
> *Why do we judge others?
>
> What does it feel like to be the judge?
>
> What does it feel like to be judged?
>
> In what sense is Jesus correct in asserting "for with the judgment you make, you will be judged?"

Focus on 7:3–5

> *What is the effect of the exaggerated word-picture in verses 3–5?
>
> How is Jesus using this humorous picture to address his hearers' blindness about themselves?

Final Discussion

> How does a person who is judgmental towards others view life and even God?

Yale University, where Professor Niebuhr had taught.

17. Bonhoeffer, *Discipleship*, 172.

*What happens to a community where people continually find fault with one another?

*Why are Jesus' words really good news for a community of faith?

Exercises:

1) Invite two volunteers to do a role-play of a married couple or two friends. The facilitator secretly instructs each person to "find fault" with his or her partner as much as possible in a five-minute period. After this time of fault-finding, stop the role-play and instruct the two volunteers to be considerate and affirming with each other for a few minutes. Finally, discuss the experience with the entire group and the two participants to discover how they were feeling during the role-play and what they learned.

2) A possible closing exercise: The facilitator invites others to close their eyes and share their prayerful responses to the proposition: *If we humans were not judgmental towards others, the world would be . . . ?* (each participant completes the sentence). After all participants have had opportunity to respond, the facilitator closes with a prayer, asking God to keep them from acting as judges of others and ending with an announcement of the good news in Rom 8:1—"There is therefore now no condemnation for those who are in Christ Jesus."

3) As another possible closing exercise, have participants stand in a circle. The facilitator shares briefly what is appreciated about the person to the right. Then that person shares words of appreciation about the next person and so on, until it comes back to the one who began the process. Then reverse the order, sharing positive comments about the person to the left until everyone is included.

Songs:

"Help Us Accept Each Other" (GTG, 766; TNCH, 388; TPH, 358; TUMH, 560; W&R, 596)

"Healer of Our Every Ill" (ELW, 612; GTG, 795; STF, 2213; TFWS, 2213; WOV, 738; W&R, 630)

"Our Father, We Have Wandered" (ELW, 606; WOV, 733; W&R, 371).

"We Are Called" (ELW, 720; STF, 2172; TFWS, 2172)

"Will You Come and Follow Me" (ELW, 798; GTG, 726; STF, 2130; TFWS, 2130; W&R, 350)

"O Christ, the Healer" (LBW, 360; GTG, 793; TNCH, 175; TPH, 380; TUMH, 265; W&R, 638)

"Let There Be Peace on Earth" (TUMH, 431; W&R, 614)

"O Christ the Same" (ELW, 760; WOV, 778; W&R, 433)—can be sung to tune Londonderry Air

Prayers:

O merciful God, we are grateful that there is no condemnation for those who are in Christ. Draw us again and again into the warmth of your amazing grace, and keep us from being judges of others. Rather give us the courage to be honest about ourselves and gracious in our relationships with others. In the name of Jesus, who came that we might enjoy life together. Amen.

Or you may choose to use the prayer circle to close your session (see Appendix, page 159).

13

Blessed Community
—Discerning Prayerfully

MATTHEW 7:7-12

7:7 *Ask, and it will be given you;*
   search, and you will find;
   knock, and the door will be opened for you.

7:8 *For everyone who asks receives,*
   and everyone who searches finds,
   and for everyone who knocks, the door will be opened.

7:9 *Is there anyone among you who,*
   if your child asks for bread, will give a stone?

7:10 *Or if the child asks for a fish, will give a snake?*

7:11 *If you then, who are evil,*
   know how to give good gifts to your children,
   how much more will your Father in heaven
   give good things to those who ask him!

7:12 *In everything do to others as you would have them do to you;*
   for this is the law and the prophets.

GETTING INTO THE TEXT

Placed immediately after a puzzling saying in 7:6 and before the Golden Rule in 7:12, this memorable passage in 7:7–11 unfolds in four segments: a three-fold exhortation and promise (7:7), a three-fold declaration as the basis for the asking and seeking (7:8), two illustrations—structured as rhetorical questions—regarding a parent responding to a child's request (7:9–10), and a conclusion built on a "how much more" comparison between a human parent and the heavenly Father (7:11).

In 7:7, the three imperatives are second person plural ("all of you") aimed at a community, not individuals. The author of Matthew would have understood these words of Jesus as addressing the corporate concerns of his hearers. Rhetorically, these paralleled exhortations (*ask, search, knock*) intensify the action needed by the community, with the two future passive verbs ("it will be given you" [*by God*] . . . "and the door will be opened for you" [*by God*]) implying the promised fulfillment from God. Then, in 7:8, the second triad repeats the same content in positive statements, reassuring the hearers of God's responsiveness to their needs.

In light of the final verse of this text (7:11, including "give" and "ask") it is usually concluded that the exhortations and promises in 7:7–8 encourage confidence in the activity of prayer, but some scholars contend that the passage focuses more narrowly on God's willingness to supply wisdom in response to communal discernment.[1] The language of "seeking and finding" reflects the wisdom tradition. For example, personified wisdom in Proverbs says "I love those who love me, and those who seek me diligently find me" (Prov 8:17). Wisdom is described as "easily discerned by those who love her, and is found by those who seek her" (Wis 6:12).

The logic of the sequence of units in 7:1–12 appears confusing, especially since the isolated saying in 7:6 seems to have no connection to what precedes and follows it ("Do not give what is holy to dogs; and do not throw your pearls before swine, or they will trample them under foot and turn and maul you"). Charles Talbert, however, suggests a progression of thought in 7:1–12 in his support of 7:7–11 as promising answers to prayers for discernment. He proposes that the saying in 7:6 pertains to Jesus' saying in 7:1–5 about "Do not judge . . ." by establishing the community's need to distinguish between holy things and what is unclean. While members of the faith community are to avoid judgmental behavior

---

1. See Talbert, *Reading,* 133–36, and Betz, *Sermon,* 506–8.

towards one another, they must "make appropriate moral judgments and distinctions and act accordingly."[2] This may include discerning that certain people are hardened against the preaching and teaching of the church. The exhortations and promises in 7:7–11 urge the community to pray for *discernment* whenever the distinction between the holy and unholy is not readily apparent. Finally, the Golden Rule in 7:12 accents the caring spirit with which the community undertakes its prayer for discernment. Talbert summarizes the logic of 7:1–12: "So far the thought has run: judge appropriately and act rightly; if you do not know how, ask God for wisdom and it will be provided; and when judging and evaluating, do it in the spirit of the Golden Rule."[3]

The wisdom tradition rests on the assumption that everyday experiences teach us a great deal. In 7:9–11, the analogy drawn from the experience of human parents with their children seeks to confirm positive outcomes for discernment prayers. The two questions expect "no" answers ("Is there anyone among you who, if your child asks for bread, will give a stone? Or if the child asks for a fish, will give a snake?"), thereby insisting that human parents do what is good for their children, not what is harmful. The child trusts the parent. For a father or mother to respond in any other way would be unthinkable.

This brings us to the conclusion of the rhetorical argumentation in 7:7–11. The "then" or "therefore" (7:11) indicates that this final verse logically builds on the previous two examples. As in 6:26 and 6:30, Jesus employs "from the lesser to the greater" method of reasoning: "If you *then*, who are evil, know how to give good gifts to your children, *how much more* will your Father in heaven give good things to those who ask him!" Based on the trustworthiness of humans in responding to their children even though they are evil, Jesus' hearers are assured of the much greater degree to which they can trust God to respond to their requests positively.

It is noteworthy that the much-repeated Golden Rule in 7:12,[4] together with 5:17, serves as the literary frame for most of the SM. Between

---

2. Talbert, *Reading*, 134.

3. Ibid., 135.

4. The Golden Rule was known in various forms throughout the ancient world. Its negative formulation occurs in a story about Rabbis Shammai and Hillel, where as in 7:12 it is also equated with the whole Torah. In the presence of Rabbi Shammai, a Gentile heathen said he would convert to Judaism if the rabbi could teach him the entire Torah while the man stood on one foot. Shammai rebuked him. Rabbi Hillel,

5:17, which declares that Jesus came to fulfill the law and the prophets, and 7:12, which asserts that the Golden Rule sums up the core of the law and the prophets, Jesus' way of interpreting the will of God is disclosed for us.

The radical notion of love espoused in the SM can relate to all human experience—our own and that of those not a part of the Christian community. The Golden Rule has the effect of universalizing the ethics of the SM. It allows *everyone* to see the reasonableness of Jesus' teaching, even its demanding call to love enemies. *We know how to act towards others, even enemies, because we know how we want them to behave towards us.* Ulrich Luz writes: "What you wish for yourself may be helpful in discovering the behavior that love demands in an actual situation. The Sermon on the Mount is not a bundle of prescriptions that legally obligate the Christian. Finally, it points to the fact that the horizon of Christian activity is universal: *human beings* are the partners. The Sermon on the Mount is by no means concerned with an ethics which is to be practiced only in the protected inner space of the Christian community."[5]

Nonetheless, practicing the Golden Rule, and hence the SM, is risky since the knowledge of what we want done for us is often overruled by self-serving motives that prompt us to act in ways that harm others. The simplicity of the Golden Rule is deceptive. It is actually radical for a community to live out such a vision!

KNOWING THE CULTURAL CONTEXT

Chapter 18 in Matthew, a discourse section also addressing directly the community's life-together, includes in verses 15–20 Jesus' words promising his presence in the midst of the community's discernment about a wayward fellow Christian.

> [15] If another member of the church sins against you, go and point out the fault when the two of you are alone. If the member listens to you, you have regained that one. [16] But if you are not listened to, take one or two others along with you, so that every word may be confirmed by the evidence of two or three witnesses. [17] If the member refuses to listen to them, tell it to the church; and if the offender refuses to listen even to the church, let such

on the other hand, in response to the same request tells the man the Golden Rule and declares, "Go and learn it." See Luz, *Matthew*, 426.

5. Luz, *Matthew*, 431.

a one be to you as a Gentile and a tax collector. [18] Truly I tell you, whatever you bind on earth will be bound in heaven, and whatever you loose on earth will be loosed in heaven. [19] Again, truly I tell you, if two of you agree on earth about anything you ask, it will be done for you by my Father in heaven. [20] For where two or three are gathered in my name, I am there among them.

Invariably Jesus' words in 18:19 are interpreted as a general promise about prayer, that is, whenever community members *agree about anything* for which they are praying, then God will grant that request. Yet this promise is placed in a literary sequence immediately after Jesus' words about binding and loosing (18:18) and directly before the promise of Jesus' presence when two or three gather in his name—a promise connected by the word "for," indicating the reason for the previous assurance (18:20). The guiding presence of Risen Jesus among them is at work in the community's prayer to God (see 28:20).

Moreover, the whole of 18:18–20 follows straightway the three-fold pattern for restoring a disobedient brother or sister to community life. So it makes more sense to interpret the prayer-promise in 18:19 in the following way: this promise is not a general one about prayer but more narrowly related to a gathering of the community's representatives as they are guided by the presence of the Risen Jesus to deliberate prayerfully regarding disputes over an errant fellow Christian. Will that member be restored to community or excluded? Are there signs of the person's repentance? In sum, Jesus' promise about prayer in 18:18 is integral to *a process of discernment about community discipline.*

The framing texts for 18:15–20, playing a similar role to the Golden Rule in 7:1–12, point to the graciousness of God. The parable of the lost sheep in 18:10–14 with the shepherd's unbounded joy at finding the lost one, Peter's question about the frequency for forgiving a brother (18:21–22), and the parable of the unmerciful servant in 18:23–35 testify to the abundance of divine mercy that shapes how humans relate to one another. The community's ministry of intervention with wayward members is to be surrounded by the incredible graciousness of God, allowing intervention to be done for the restoration of the brother or sister and for the health of the community, not in a vindictive spirit. Thus, communal discernment is necessary but is coupled with *concern* and *love* for those being evaluated. This is a pattern similar to what occurs in 7:1–12—the *prayer for discernment* over what is holy and unclean (7:7–11) is to be undertaken with the *kindness and wisdom of the Golden Rule* in mind (7:12).

ENGAGING THE TEXT TODAY

If, as in 18:15–20, the strong encouragement to pray with the assurance of God's responsiveness in 7:7–11 is directed to the community's task of discernment, then 7:7–8 is not intended as a general promise about prayer. An open-ended pledge by God to grant the community's every request could lead to dangerous and self-serving notions of prayer within the community.

It makes far more sense that the passages in both chapters 7 and 18 support the very real ministry of discernment faced by the faith community on many occasions. More than once, the apostle Paul speaks to this communal task of discernment. In 1 Thess 5:21–22 Paul counsels *"but test everything*; hold fast to what is good; abstain from every form of evil," and in Rom 12:2: "Do not be conformed to this world, but be transformed by the renewing of your minds, *so that you may discern what is the will of God*—what is good and acceptable and perfect." In both texts, the Greek word (*dokimazein*), translated "test" and "discern" respectively, means "to make a critical examination of something to determine genuineness" or "to draw a conclusion about worth on the basis of testing."[6] Elsewhere in Rom. 16:17–18, Paul warns: "I urge you, brothers and sisters, to keep an eye on those who cause dissensions and offenses, in opposition to the teaching that you have learned; avoid them. For such people do not serve our Lord Christ, but their own appetites, and by smooth talk and flattery they deceive the hearts of the simple-minded."[7]

In their environment, early Christian congregations often faced difficult decisions as to whether or not the behavior of certain persons was in line with God's will. Christian communities sometimes had to deal with outsiders who were trying to take advantage of believers, often doing so in deceptive ways. Matthew 7:15–23 speaks of "false prophets, who come to you in sheep's clothing but inwardly are ravenous wolves." Whoever these false prophets were, they were not welcomed in the Matthean community because of their conniving intent.

Today many are talking and writing about *discernment* as a practice needed in Christian communities. This emphasis on discernment is in part a reaction to the Robert's Rules of Order model employed in most congregational and governing meetings of churches that allows little

---

6. *BDAG*, 255–56.

7. See also Heb 5:14: "But solid food is for the mature, for those whose faculties have been trained by practice to distinguish good from evil."

space for contemplation of Scripture and listening prayer in decision making. According to Martin Copenhaver, these rules were developed by Henry Robert in 1876 as a result of his frustration over a church meeting that dragged on with no way to resolve differences. Copenhaver writes further: "To be sure, following Robert's Rules can make meetings efficient. But it creates other problems. It ignores spiritual practices. By elevating the principle of 'one person, one vote,' the emphasis is squarely on the individual view and on the sum of individuals' votes. It creates winners and losers of votes. The process is slanted in favor of those who know the rules and can manipulate them."[8]

What would it mean for congregations and other gatherings of Christians, without jettisoning all parliamentary rules, to think more intentionally about the practice of *communal discernment?* We have few clues from New Testament times regarding the actual practice of communal discernment. We do know, however, that the earliest Christians trusted that the Spirit was powerfully active among them and that praying opened them to God's direction and wisdom.

Put simply, "Discernment is a way of listening and paying attention to God's leading."[9] Practicing discernment together puts a premium on *listening*—listening for God's leading in prayer, listening prayerfully to scriptural texts, and listening respectfully to others committed with us to deliberate about matters important to the life and mission of the faith community. We hear God's voice through prayer and Scripture but also by listening to others. Recall that the central declaration of the Jewish faith is "Hear, O Israel" (the *Shema* in Deut 6:4) where the emphasis is on listening and not talking.

To become intentional in our listening means becoming more comfortable with silence. Listening is difficult, an art not frequently fostered in our combative, talkative culture. It requires more time and a focus on central issues. We can learn from the Quaker tradition to train leaders in listening and practicing silence, in shaping meetings to be "listening meetings" where silence plays an important role in listening to one another and thereby to the leading of God. "In the context of the group discernment process, how do we know when we are to speak? The short answer is that we must speak when and only when God tells us to speak

---

8. Copenhaver, "Decide or Discern," 29.

9. Definition given in Isenhower and Todd, *Listen*, 11.

. . . This may mean speaking much less frequently than we are accustomed to doing."[10]

The words of Jesus in 7:7–11 provide the needed encouragement for the community to keep active and optimistic in its search for faithful answers and just solutions to the dilemmas of its life together. They are to trust that "asking" does lead to "receiving," "seeking" does lead to "finding," and "knocking" on doors does cause them to be "opened." The *contrast community* is a praying and listening community that remains upbeat about life and about the gracious God who authors and supplies all good things.

DWELLING IN THE TEXT

Quotes:

- "Discernment does not simply confirm our hunches or intuitions. Instead, it is a perilous practice that involves self-criticism, questions, and risk—and it often redirects our lives."[11]

- "Rather, discernment is 'serious reflection on scripture, grounded in prayer and informed by experience. It is both deeply personal and entirely communal.'"[12]

- "Sometimes I think we do all the talking because we are afraid God won't. Or, conversely, that God will. Either way, staying preoccupied with our own words seems a safer bet than opening ourselves up either to God's silence or God's speech, both of which have the power to undo us."[13]

- "In a time of famine typified by too many words with too much noise in them, we could use fewer words with more silence in them."[14]

---

10. As stated in Copenhaver's review "Decide or Discern," when the author is quoting *Practicing Discernment Together* by Lon Fendall, Jan Wood, and Bruce Bishop. In the final chapters of this book, Jan Wood offers concrete suggestions for a leader in guiding a community's discernment regarding a specific issue (95–118).

11. Bass, *Christianity*, 95.

12. Ibid., 92, quoting Robert, who was attending an Episcopal church in California.

13. Taylor, *When God is Silent*, 51.

14. Ibid., 113.

Questions for Discussions:

The starred questions may be selected when the session is shorter than an hour.

*How have you understood the meaning of this passage?

*What do you think is the purpose of praying?

*Is it a new idea for you to describe prayer as having to do more with listening than making requests? Why or why not?

How would you design meetings in your congregation or faith community to allow more time for discerning God's leading in the matters under discussion?

Are you a good listener? Why or why not?

*What makes for good listening to others and to God?

How comfortable are you with silence—even the silence of God?

*Why is it crucial to remember the Golden Rule (7:12) when you are discerning together God's leading in making a decision?

*How might your congregation use the process of discernment to ponder the implications of Jesus' teaching in the SM for your life together?

Exercises:

1) Discuss one or more of the quotes above.

2) Divide into subgroups of four to six persons and assign to each group a discussion topic pertinent to the life and mission of your faith community. The first speaker holds an object that can be passed (e.g., a cross or a Bible or a candle). After sharing regarding the issue, the first person then hands the object to a second group member, who begins by briefly summarizing the first speaker's thoughts. In turn, the second person shares and passes the object to the next person, who summarizes what the second speaker has said before he or she speaks. This process continues until all have shared, and the first speaker has summarized the last speaker's comments (fifteen to twenty minutes).

Songs:

"Lord, Listen to Your Children Praying" (ELW, 752; GTG, 469; WOV, 775; STF, 2193; TFBF, 247; TFWS, 2193; W&R, 489)

"Here, O Lord, Your Servants Gather" (ELW, 530; GTG, 311; TPH, 465; TUMH, 552; W&R, 597)

"Seek Ye First the Kingdom of God" (WOV, 783; GTG, 175; TFBF, 149; TH1982, 711; TPH, 333; TUMH, 405; W&P, 122; W&R, 349).

"God Is Waiting For Us" (BC, 2:535)

"Rise Up, O Saints of God!" (ELW, 669; LBW, 383; TH1982, 551; TUMH, 576; W&R, 590)—especially verses 1 and 5

"Nothing Can Trouble" (GTG, 820; STF, 2054; TFWS, 2054; W&R, 421)

"Lord, Speak to Us, That We May Speak" (ELW, 676; GTG, 722; LBW, 403; TNCH, 531; TUMH, 463; W&R, 593)

Prayers:

O Listening God, give us the humility and patience to listen to you and to others. Slow us down and give us your peace. Teach us to be silent in order to discern your word to us. In the name of Jesus Christ, the Word spoken out of silence. Amen.

You may also choose to use the prayer circle to close your session (see Appendix, page 159).

14

Blessed Community —Building on Solid Rock

MATTHEW 7:24-27

24 *Everyone then who hears these words of mine and acts on them*
   will be like a wise man who built his house on rock.

25 *The rain fell,*
   the floods came,
   and the winds blew and beat on that house,
   but it did not fall, because it had been founded on rock.

26 *And everyone who hears these words of mine*
               and does not act on them
   will be like a foolish man who built his house on sand.

27 *The rain fell,*
   and the floods came,
    and the winds blew and beat against that house,
     and it fell—and great was its fall!"

GETTING INTO THE TEXT

This brief picture-narrative of two men building on rock and sand completes a sequence of contrasts at the end of the SM (two gates/roads, two trees, and two foundations). Each segment confronts the hearers with dramatic alternatives associated with the end-times. They are to choose the difficult and less frequented way that leads to life, not the broad and easy one that leads to destruction (7:13–14); they are to watch out for "false prophets" in their midst by evaluating these leaders' behavior since the good tree produces good fruit, not bad (7:15–23); and they are to build their lives on a solid foundation by hearing and putting into practice these teachings of Jesus in the SM (7:24–27).

Matthew 7:28–29, the final two verses in the SM, call to mind the opening verses in 5:1–2. There the narrator informs the listeners that Jesus, upon seeing the crowds, climbs the mountain, sits down, and teaches his disciples who approach him. This seems to imply that Jesus' teaching in the SM is intended only for disciples, not the crowds. Yet the closing verses in 7:28–29 plainly note that the crowds not only hear Jesus' words but are also deeply affected by them, recognizing an authority in Jesus' teaching that surpasses that of the scribes who teach the Torah. This bracketing of the SM with 5:1–2 and 7:28–29 indicates that Matthew intends that the Christians of his day appreciate that Jesus' kingdom teaching is open to all. The circle of disciples is incomplete, and Jesus' world-shattering words constantly invite crowds into the disciplined and joyous life of the Christian community.

According to Hans Dieter Betz, "the use of building metaphors to end an *epitome* of this kind is stylistically traditional."[1] A similar form of this short parable of two builders also concludes Luke's Sermon on the Plain (Luke 6:20–49). A rhetorical question begins the final section in Luke 6:46–49 to warn Jesus' disciples to put into practice his foundational teachings ("Why do you call me 'Lord, Lord,' and do not do what I tell you?"). It is *hearing and acting* on the words of Jesus that is crucial. The Lukan version of the building parable focuses on the process undertaken by the prudent builder. The man building a house takes time and energy to dig down deep through the soil to lay the foundation on rock. The other man builds his house without unearthing a proper foundation.

---

1. Betz, *Sermon*, 637. Note that an *epitome* designates a summary collection of the teaching of prominent person in antiquity. For further explanation, see chapter 1, p. 4.

The Matthean rendering of this word-picture, on the other hand, does not contain the Lukan details of insuring a rock underpinning for the house. It offers a simple contrast between "a wise man who built his house on rock" (7:24) and "a foolish man who built his house on sand" (7:26). Both verses begin with the word *everyone,* an all-embracing pronoun that excludes no one from a choice about Jesus' teaching in the SM. Everyone listening must decide whether or not they will take Jesus' words so seriously that they will actually *do them.* The contrast is entirely clear. The wise builder both *hears and acts on* these words of Jesus in the SM. The foolish one, by contrast, *hears and does not act on* the words of Jesus. The failure to practice the SM makes all the difference. The two Greek adjectives used to characterize the builders contrast practical wisdom (*phronimos*) with stupid behavior (*mōros*).[2]

The difference lies with the foundation on which each house is built—rock or sandy subsoil. The house built on sand cannot withstand the heavy winds and torrential rains that cause a sudden, raging rush of water through the Palestinian valleys in the winter season. Unlike the house built on rock, the house built on sand does not hold firm but collapses. The last few words of this stark comparison underscore the utter tragedy befalling the house of the foolish builder—"and great was its fall" (7:27). Hearers are left with this ominous warning.

This dramatic word-picture in 7:24–27 brings the hearers full circle. Early in the SM we heard that the blessed ones are those who "hunger and thirst for [God's] righteousness" (5:6) and practice that righteousness so completely that their actions get them into trouble (5:10–11). Now the foolish who do not follow Jesus' teachings suffer the consequences. From the opening verses to the close, the SM invites a community to do more than listen to Jesus' teaching; it invites that community to *practice* it. Ulrich Luz states, "*In* this practice, there is the experience of grace and prayer. This is what the Sermon on the Mount proclaims from the Beatitudes to the conclusion. Standing or falling in the judgment depends on this praxis."[3]

2. See *BDAG,* 663, 1066.

3. Luz, *Matthew,* 454.

KNOWING THE CULTURAL CONTEXT

The biblical peoples knew the importance of building a house on a rock foundation. Unlike today's world, there were no backhoes to dig deep into the ground or cement mixers to pour and form firm concrete footings for a building. Kenneth Bailey, who has lived and taught New Testament for forty years in the Middle East, offers cultural insights regarding this brief parable of the two builders easily missed by most Western Christians.[4] He points to the time and effort involved in building a house in ancient Palestine. A person would undertake this strenuous construction project only in the summer or dry season, because the rainy winter would make it impossible to proceed due to mud and sloppy conditions. In Palestine, the rainy season lasts from November to April or May. The summer months of June through October would offer dry, warm, and sunny days for building. But, as Bailey also notes, the summer's hot sun bakes the clay-like soil and makes it "like bronze" (quoting Lev 26:19). He writes descriptively:

> It is easy to imagine a builder in summer, with little imagination or wisdom, thinking that he can build an adequate one-level house on hard clay. With his pick he tries digging and finds the ground is indeed "like bronze." The walls will not be more than seven feet high. It is hot. The idea of long days of backbreaking work under a hot, cloudless sky does not appeal to him. He opts to build his simple one- or two-room home on the hardened clay. The underlying rock is down there somewhere—it will all work out! He constructs a roof with a reasonable overhang and is pleased that he has managed to finish before the onset of the rains.[5]

But the rains do come and can produce flash floods that turn the dry hardened clay into mucky and spongy soil, allowing settling and the buckling of the stonewalls of a house. A house constructed of uncut fieldstones and mud mortar without a firm foundation quite easily collapses in torrential conditions as one stone and then another pops out until the walls cave in. It is absolutely crucial to build the house on bedrock.

> The prudent, hardworking builder knows better. In the Holy Land solid rock lies everywhere—just beneath the soil. If the builder plans a house in a valley, the earth and rubble may be

4. See Bailey, *Jesus,* 321–31.
5. Ibid., 323.

ten or more feet deep. On the tops of the low hills the underlying rock is barely covered and often exposed. I have asked numerous village builders about the depth they must excavate to construct a stone house. The answer is always the same. They tell me they must dig "down to the rock." If that means one inch or ten feet, the principle remains the same. Building must be done *on the rock.*[6]

This necessary foundation stone is mentioned in a number of biblical passages. 1 Kings 5:17, for example, describes the quarrying and dressing of large stones for the foundation of the temple when Solomon was king of Israel ("At the king's command, they quarried out great, costly stones in order to lay the foundation of the house with dressed stones"). *Foundation stone* can also be used metaphorically as in Isa 28:16 when Israel is under a threat from the Assyrian armies—"therefore thus says the Lord God, See, I am laying in Zion a foundation stone, a tested stone, a precious cornerstone, a sure foundation: 'One who trusts will not panic.'"[7] In 1 Cor 3:10–11, Paul uses the image to speak of Jesus Christ as the foundation stone that he as a *wise builder* has laid and on which others must build ("According to the grace of God given to me, like a skilled master builder I laid a foundation, and someone else is building on it. Each builder must choose with care how to build on it. For no one can lay any foundation other than the one that has been laid; that foundation is Jesus Christ"). The Book of Job also uses the example of an unsound foundation to depict the vulnerability of the wicked before God: "They were snatched away before their time; their foundation was washed away by a flood" (Job 22:16).

Although it is the Lukan version that makes explicit this more prudent and demanding building process, Matt 7:24–27 does state the fundamental choice facing the builder. Where does one build his house—on rock or sand? Analogously the audience, then and now, hearing the SM is faced with a decisive alternative. Do they build their lives on Jesus and his words—the sure foundation—or do they give Jesus and his words only passing consideration? The placement of this building parable at the conclusion of the SM (and the Sermon on the Plain in Luke 6:17–49) underscores this monumental decision.

6. Ibid., 324.

7. Bailey, 324–27, argues persuasively that Isa 28:14–18 is the prophetic passage whose history of use lies behind Luke 6:46–49 (and Matt 7:24–27).

ENGAGING THE TEXT TODAY

We conclude our engagement with Jesus' teachings in the SM where we started. We are invited to *hear* and *understand* these words, but we are also to *do* them. As the subtitle to this book indicates, *Practicing the Sermon on the Mount* is the challenge, both for the earliest followers and for faith-communities today. Jesus' parable of the two builders in 7:24–27 ends the SM with promise and warning: all who *hear* these words of Jesus and *do* them establish their lives on a sure foundation, whereas all who *only hear* and *do not practice* these words build their lives on shaky soil unable to withstand the storms of existence. The prudent choice to build on Jesus' teachings demands energy and effort.

To lay emphasis on the *practice* of the SM is not to dismiss the *hearing* of these words as inconsequential. We live in a time when many people are involved in numerous commitments that result in a hurried lifestyle with little time for listening and learning. Even Christians may take little time for deep pondering of the larger Scriptures or just the words of Jesus.

A group of committed persons can move towards understanding and appropriation of Jesus' teachings through *dialogue* with the SM and with one another. Hans Dieter Betz argues forcefully that the SM is designed as a summary of Jesus' teaching to sponsor discussion and even debate. "Furthermore, 'hearing' implies a dialogical structure of the teaching. This structure means that, although the SM is presented as a monologue of Jesus, its structure is that of a dialogue. It provokes debate, both among the disciples and internally in the individual. The dialogical structure is therefore considered to be an essential element of the teaching of Jesus."[8] Betz's insight carries implication for our engagement with the SM. *Hearing* these teachings of Jesus is not a matter of simply physically hearing them and then being able to repeat them. It is a matter of discussing them, debating them, and together attempting to make sense of them in our own contexts. This process of grappling with the SM is essential in a group's movement towards practice. The interaction of reflection and practice deepens the understanding of Jesus and his kingdom teaching. This study, particularly the "Dwelling in the Text" segment, has been designed to foster this deeper engagement with the SM.

---

8. Betz, *Sermon*, 561.

"The teachings cannot be severed from the deed, but neither can the deeds be severed from the teachings!"[9] These words of Martin Buber underscore the integral connection between teaching and deeds. Christians can grow by taking time to ponder seriously the implications of Jesus' teaching for the character of their congregation and for their own daily living. The SM addresses the human propensity to separate what they hear from what they do.

The SM calls us into a way of righteousness and justice that *can* be expressed in human attitudes and actions. It is not an impossible ideal. Jesus calls us to give close attention to all he has taught (28:20), the concrete will of God that he himself lived out in the fullest manner (5:17). Although the SM does not in fact speak of "believing in Jesus," it does assume that the person and earthly ministry of Jesus (including his crucifixion and resurrection) underlay the teachings. It is this crucified and risen Jesus who continues to speak and engage the community of faith through his words. The crucified and risen Jesus becomes the source of grace and courage for the communal journey in *hearing* and *doing* the SM. We sense, often quite feebly, that Jesus' person and teaching are the bedrock foundation on which we must build.

At the beginning of this treatment of the SM, I quoted from Dietrich Bonhoeffer that the Bible and especially the SM rescued him from a self-absorbed way of living. We turn to Bonhoeffer again as we conclude our engagement with the SM. These comments were written at the end of his interpretation of the SM:

> We have heard the Sermon on the Mount; perhaps we have understood it. But who has heard it correctly? Jesus answers this question last. Jesus does not permit his listeners to simply walk away, making whatever they like of his discourse, extracting what seems to them to be useful in their lives, testing how this teaching compares to "reality." Jesus does not deliver his word up to his listeners, so that it is misused in their rummaging hands. Instead, he gives it to them in a way that it alone retains power over them. From the human point of view there are countless possibilities of understanding and interpreting the Sermon on the Mount. Jesus knows only one possibility: simply go and obey. Do not interpret or apply, but do it and obey. That is the only way Jesus' word is really heard. But again, doing something

9. Buber, *Israel and the World*, 144.

is not to be understood as an ideal possibility; instead, we are simply to begin acting.[10]

DWELLING IN THE TEXT

Quotes:

- With this parable Jesus placed upon his congregation the tremendous responsibility of classifying themselves. Their response to *these* words of his would determine whether they were wise men or idiots. He had given them the kingdom manifesto, had described the kingdom citizen, proclaimed the kingdom standards of righteousness, offered the kingdom of God *on earth* as a specific proposal for a new world order. Now he lays it squarely in their laps. Will they accept it or reject it? Will they hear it and praise it, or hear it and build it? In brief, will they wisely repent or foolishly continue in their same old order?[11]

- We have already indicated that in our case teaching is inseparably bound up with doing. Here, if anywhere, it is impossible to teach or to learn without living. The teachings must not be treated as a collection of knowable material; they resist such treatment. Either the teachings live in the life of a responsible human being, or they are not alive at all. The teachings do not center in themselves; they do not exist for their own sake. They refer to, they are directed toward the deed. In this connection the concept of "deed" does not, of course, connote "activism," but life that realizes the teachings in the changing potentialities of every hour.[12]

Questions:

For brief sessions, use only the starred questions.

Why does it seem appropriate to end the SM with the parable of the two builders?

10. Bonhoeffer, *Discipleship*, 181.
11. Jordan, *Sermon*, 123.
12. Buber, *Israel and the World*, 140.

*How does knowledge about building conditions in ancient Palestine alter your understanding of 7:24–27?

*The coming of rain is most often a blessing, but heavy rains resulting in flooding conditions can be devastating and destructive. Has your area every experienced the destructive force of flooding waters? If so, describe what happened and how it made you feel. Did it change how you lived and planned?

*How closely linked are *hearing* and *understanding* to actually being able to *act*?

Can you give an example of a time when your activity led you to understand a situation or a task more deeply?

Do the words of Martin Buber quoted above trigger any more thoughts about the text?

How is practicing the SM different from what Buber calls "activism?"

*What teachings of Jesus in the SM are most challenging for you to practice?

In what way does your understanding and practice of the SM relate to end-time judgment?

*What is implied by stating that the person and ministry of Jesus (including his crucifixion and resurrection) empower our practice of his teaching in the SM?

*How has this engagement with the Sermon on the Mount changed you and prompted you to behave differently?

Exercises:

1) Divide the group into subgroups to plan and enact the parable of the two builders. Allow five minutes for the planning and then invite the subgroups to act out the brief story, even providing sound effects where appropriate. Then discuss briefly what they learned by doing this exercise.

2) Working in pairs, take eight minutes to discuss how you would put into practice one particular teaching of Jesus. Invite all to share briefly with the full group what was learned about the SM and themselves by this exercise.

3) As follow-up exercise to the study, form a working group to review what the participants learned during their engagement with the SM and to consider the following: a) *How do you evaluate the life and activity*

of your congregation in light of Jesus' teachings in the SM? b) What is a strategy for assisting the congregation in embodying more teachings of the SM?

Songs:

"Build Your Faith" (BC, 2:556)

"My Hope is Built on Nothing Less" (ELW, 597; GTG, 353; LBW, 293, 294; TFBF, 192; TNCH, 403; TPH, 379; TUMH, 368; W&R, 405)

"My Life Flows On in Endless Song" (ELW, 763; GTG, 821; STF, 2212; TFWS, 2212; TNCH, 476; WOV, 781; W&R, 424)

"If You Will Trust in God to Guide You" (ELW, 769; GTG, 816; LBW, 453; TH1982, 635; TNCH, 410; TPH, 282; TUMH, 142; W&R, 429)

"Take My Life, That I May Be" (ELW, 685; GTG, 679; LBW, 406; TH1982, 707; TNCH, 448; TPH, 391; TUMH, 399; W&R, 466)

"We Would Be Building" (TNCH, 607)

"Built on a Rock" (LBW, 365; W&R, 546; W&S, 3147)

"The Church's One Foundation" (LBW, 369; GTG, 321; TH1982, 525; TNCH, 386; TPH, 442; TUMH, 545; W&R, 545)

Prayer:

Sovereign God, in Jesus you place before us the way of life. We thank you for this gracious gift in the person and passion of Jesus. Give us the wisdom and courage to follow him and his teachings as the life-giving way of your kingdom here on earth. In his merciful name we pray. Amen.

Appendix

A Strategy for Dwelling in the Word

ALTHOUGH IT IS THE Spirit of God who effects change within us and our community, it does not happen without our involvement. This description of "Dwelling in the Word"[1] serves as an explanation of the process employed in this book. These guidelines can prove useful to pastors and lay leaders who choose to develop a similar process for engaging other biblical texts.

It takes intentionality and time for a community of Christians to be transformed by the SM or other biblical texts. Fleeting attention to Jesus' teaching or other passages does not typically alter the basic culture of a congregation—how its members view life, relate to one another, employ their time and money, approach challenges and conflicts, and manage their daily routines. For example, participants in a faith community need to *dwell in* Jesus' words in the SM—to hear them, learn them, understand them, discuss them, ponder them, take them seriously, even risk doing them—in order to change. By dwelling in these texts, Christians risk trusting Jesus' kingdom message in the midst of a world that seems to operate so differently. In doing so, twenty-first-century Christians place themselves in a position somewhat similar to the earliest followers of Jesus, who *heard* rather than *read* Jesus' words. The process can also apply to other texts.

1. This phrase is used in the Partnership for Missional Church process developed by Church Innovations Institute (directed by Patrick Keifert) to describe the practice of repeatedly hearing, pondering, and discussing key biblical passages. After nearly two decades, CI leaders have concluded that this practice of *dwelling in the text* is the "most significant innovation" in prompting renewed and mission-oriented congregations. See Keifert, *We*, 68–71.

Prior to the written Gospels, it was the oral tradition that served as the primary mode among the earliest Christians for sharing the *remembered* stories about Jesus and *remembered* words of his teaching. One scholar describes such an *oral tradition* "as a corporate memory giving identity to the group which thus remembers."[2] This *communal remembering* began already during the ministry of Jesus but also continued in the post-Easter church, noticeably shaped by the believers' experience of the ongoing presence and guidance of the Risen Jesus.

Even after the Gospels were rendered in written form by the last third of the first century, the encounter with Jesus remained an *acoustical event* for most followers of Jesus, since few could read.[3] They *heard* the Gospels, or parts of them, read and re-read, or, as David Rhoads asserts, "orally performed."[4] They *heard* particular sayings of Jesus and stories about him shared verbally when they gathered for worship and fellowship. Certain words of Jesus were probably *heard* so often that these words gently lodged themselves in their memory. The community, for example, could *remember* Jesus' words in the SM "You are the light of the world" (Matt 5:14a) or "Do not judge, so that you may not be judged" (Matt 7:1). Repeatedly spoken and shared, these sayings and stories of Jesus entered the memory and vocabulary of the community and actually molded participants' ways of seeing and acting.

For the earliest Christians, these *remembered* words and stories were not the artifact of a Jewish rabbi and prophet, now absent from them,

---

2. Dunn, *Jesus Remembered*, 173, n. 1. Rhoads, "Performance Criticism?" 85, broadens this point by describing the New Testament oral culture: "The overwhelming 95 percent of the people were non-literate peasants or urban dwellers who experienced everything they learned aurally. Everything they learned and knew, they learned by word of mouth . . . Life was communal life. There was no individualism as we know it today. The identity of individuals came as part of their collective identity. People were always with other people, and what one person knew everybody knew. Knowledge was social knowledge because everybody talked with everybody else and everybody told stories. Memory was social memory."

3. Whitney Shiner, "Oral Performance in the New Testament World" in Hearon and Ruge-Jones, 49, asserts: "In the first century, writing was largely understood as a representation of speech. Oral communication was understood as true communication. A book was a list of words waiting to become communication."

4. Rhoads, "Performance Criticism?" 87. He states, "Therefore, the writings we have in the New Testament are examples of 'performance literature,' that is, literature that was meant for performance . . ." Using performance to teach the New Testament is a burgeoning area of interest within the academy and church. See www.biblicalperformancecriticism.org for discussions and resources.

but were the *ongoing presence* of the risen Lord Jesus, who promised to abide with them and guide them until the end of the age (Matt 28:20). His teachings were *active and dynamic words* for a community that was anticipating the complete and magnificent disclosure of God's merciful and righteous reign on earth (see Matt 6:10).

In the twenty-first century we clearly rely a great deal on written documents, yet we too appreciate the power of sound bites on TV, memorable phrases in political campaigns, slogans in advertising, lyrics in popular music. With this in mind, the questions before us include: How can we get Jesus' instructive and transformative words off the written page and released into our faith communities? How can people in a Christian community intentionally pursue a strategy that engages texts not merely as written language to be read hastily but as life-changing stories and words of the Lord Jesus to be memorized, pondered, internalized, and enacted?

METHODS FOR TRANSFORMATIVE STUDY

THERE ARE NUMEROUS APPROACHES that foster a transformative encounter with scriptural passages. These methods invite participants to slow down and spend time in dialogue with the text.

1) Retelling a passage:

Benefits accrue from learning a biblical passage by heart. A Scripture passage "learned by heart" abides with a person for pondering and reflection, for guiding and shaping decisions and activity, and for sharing freely with others. As your group engages a text, encourage at least some participants to memorize specific passages. Suggestions for the memorizing process include:[5]

- Select a good English translation (e.g., NRSV or NIV);
- Outline the passage on paper according to its narrative or logical structure;
- Review the entire passage;
- Commit its overall sequence to memory—noting time and place, characters and their interaction;

5. See Boomershine, *Story Journey*, 24–31.

- Memorize the first segment of the passage, repeating these words aloud until the segment is memorized;

- Repeat this process for each new segment until the entire passage is fixed in memory.

Early in this memorizing process, consider the various ways the words can be spoken. Make choices about inflection, emphasis, volume, tempo, facial expressions, gestures, pace, pauses, emotional tone, and bodily movement. Making these decisions about the delivery of the words compels the "performers to decide what message or impact they will convey by *how* they say each and every line with certain inflections and intonations."[6] Once the passage is memorized, practice telling it in the presence of another person or small group to gain some confidence in your ability to share the passage. Finally, do not fret if you do not perfectly repeat the passage or even forget a portion—if the overall sequence is clear in your mind, you can improvise with your own words to fill in memory gaps.

Dennis Dewey, a biblical storyteller, draws a distinction between what we normally call "memorization" and "learning by heart." Memorization can be a "head" process, while "heart-learning" engages the whole person. He states, "Good biblical storytelling is based, not on the memorization of the words of text alone, but rather in a creative act of assembling and reassembling the text from patterns and elements of its sensory images, feeling tones, and narrative contours—what we storytellers refer to as the story's 'geography.' To perform the Sermon on the Mount is have been to the mountaintop and to have glimpsed in the imagination what lies beyond."[7]

Stories about Jesus are more easily memorized than a sequence of his teaching. Nevertheless, committing key teachings to memory helps participants to attend to the details of a passage and to consider the rhetorical impact of these words when spoken. At the outset of the study, each willing participant could be assigned one portion of the SM to memorize with the goal of performing the SM aloud by the end of the sessions. Some participants may be prepared to share orally their memorized segment when it is discussed in class. Since memorizing and

6. Rhoads, "Performance Criticism?" 97–98.

7. Dewey, "Great in the Empire of Heaven: A Faithful Performance of Matthew's Sermon on the Mount," 83, in Fleer and Bland, eds., *Preaching*. See also Lee and Scott, *Sound Mapping*, 309–26, 336–46, for an analysis of "the patterned repetition of sounds" (320) that facilitated the hearing and remembering of the SM.

performing a passage is frightening for many persons, create a supportive setting to encourage some risk-taking. If class members hesitate, use the DVD of a performance of the SM by David Rhoads as a model.[8]

Memorizing Jesus' words or stories about Jesus has many benefits for both performers and hearers. Getting Jesus' words off the page enriches our understanding of them and their role in gospel narrative. Moreover, it can create community as Thomas Boomershine avows: "Storytelling creates community. Persons who tell each other stories become friends. And men and women who know the same stories deeply are bound together in special ways."[9]

2) Pondering quotes:

A saying or quote pertinent to a specific passage is worth consideration by the group. As leader, you may choose to incorporate a given quotation into the group discussion by basing a question on it. Normally including two or three quotations is sufficient for each session. You may find quotations from your own files and reading or by searching the internet.

3) Responding to questions:[10]

William Sloane Coffin Jr. once claimed that true religion is not having all the right answers but "having all the right questions."[11] Jesus himself is often depicted in the Gospel stories as posing questions—sometimes rhetorical ones designed to remind his hearers of what they should already know and sometimes penetrating questions that challenge the hearers' easy assumptions about God and life. Examples of his rhetorical

---

8. David Rhoads has orally performed various portions of the New Testament, including the SM. You can acquire a DVD of his oral performance of the SM and other portions of the New Testament from Select Learning Resources (www.selectlearning. org) by ordering "Dramatic Presentations of the New Testament" by David Rhoads. Go to the online store and click on the category New Testament to find this resource.

9. Boomershine, *Story Journey*, 18.

10. See the chapter "Developing and Using Questions" in Wink, *Transforming*, 92–100.

11. Coffin, as the chaplain at Yale University in the 1960s, was active in the civil rights struggle and a critic of church leaders who had absolute certainty about all things religious.

questions (Matt 6:25b, 26b, 27, 28) and penetrating questions (Mt. 5:13b, 46–47; 7:3) appear in the SM.

In every age, followers of Jesus are inescapably on a pilgrimage of inquiry filled with questions. That is the nature of the faith life. For this reason, it is useful to approach biblical passages with an eye to the questions raised or implied by a text. Posing and pondering questions is a sign of faithfulness—not doubt!

It is an exciting enterprise to study a text closely and then develop a series of questions for consideration in a small study group. As you initially read through a text, it is helpful to jot down all the questions that the passage prompts for you. After some serious study of that same text, you can begin narrowing your list of questions in order to select those worth posing to the group. Here are some hints for formulating questions:

- Make questions clear and simple, asking no more than one thing at a time.

- Do not ask questions that can be answered simply "yes" or "no," unless you follow up with a "why" or "why not."

- Develop questions that do not set up respondents for offering "the right answers" but invite a rich range of responses, particularly in terms of their own experiences.

- Construct questions that engage participants both intellectually and experientially.

- Attempt to move with the concreteness of the text itself in order to avoid dealing in abstractions (e.g., pose questions that explore images and symbols in the passage as well as its ironic and surprising features).

- Think of questions that are assumed by the text within its New Testament context (e.g., What problem or question within the New Testament community is being addressed?).

- Relate questions to the text's vision of God's activity, the figure of Jesus, or the way human beings think and act.

- When appropriate, employ questions that are open-ended (e.g., When you hear the word "mountain" or "desert," what visual images or scene do you see?).

Once you have developed a list of questions, consider them carefully. Select both *exploratory questions* and *engagement questions*. *Exploratory questions* invite participants to explore and understand more fully the world of the text itself within its historical and literary context. In contrast, *engagement questions* prompt them to mull over some aspect of the passage in light of their own contemporary experience, both personal and communal.

When you have arrived at a list of potential questions, plan the sequence to be used. Normally questions will trace the actual development of the text itself, ending with a few questions that assist participants in drawing together and pondering the major insights generated by the passage. It is always good to include an opening question that allows participants to comment on the text more generally without the narrowing focus of a specific question. After you develop the final list of questions (eight to ten questions for an hour's discussion and fewer questions for a shorter time), consider them yourself, pray over them, and attempt to adopt a beginner's mind in responding to the selected questions.

It is possible to utilize *lectio divina* ("divine reading"),[12] a traditional meditative way to listen to God through a particular scriptural passage. This approach encourages participants to read the text slowly at least three times and respond to a specific question after each reading. These general questions can apply to all texts: a) After the first reading, *What word or phrase captures your attention?*; b) After the second reading, *Where does this text touch our lives today?*; and c) After the final reading, *From what we have heard and shared, what is God calling us to do or be that is life-giving? How is God inviting us to change?* After the final responses, one might read the text again and close with prayer.

---

12. Quoting Judy Nolde's handout on spiritual practices prepared for the Missional Discovery Journey in the South-Central Synod of Wisconsin, Evangelical Lutheran Church in Amercia: "Latin for 'divine reading,' *lectio divina* provides a way of praying with Scripture. This is a way of reading the Bible not for information but rather with the intention of listening for God. A Bible passage is read slowly several times. The structure for *lectio* can vary, but generally it consists of four stages: *lectio*—after the first reading, say out loud any words or phrases that particularly struck you from the passage; *meditation*—after the second reading, meditate on the passage and share what it means for you; *oratio*—after the third reading, talk about whether the passage makes you want to respond in some way and *contemplatio*—after the fourth reading, rest in God."

4) Using mutual invitation:[13]

Mutual invitation is a method to ensure that everyone in the group has opportunity to share. This simple procedure prevents verbal domination by a few. The leader or a designated participant responds to the first question posed. He or she then invites another person to share (not simply the person sitting next to the inviter). After the second person has spoken, this person invites another person to respond. Each time a person is invited to respond, that person has three options: 1) share, 2) "pass" (the person does not want to speak), or 3) "pass for now" (the person has something to share but is not ready to do so). If a person says "pass for now," that participant will be invited to share later. No matter which option a person exercises, that person will proceed to invite the next participant. This continues until everyone in the group has been invited.

During a longer session of interactive conversation with a biblical passage, the leader might choose to use "mutual invitation" only one or two times, chiefly when *engagement questions* are fashioned to have participants appropriate the meaning of the text for their own personal and congregational contexts. Strategic use of mutual invitation, depending on the size of the group, can encourage all to gain their voice and hence enrich the group's conversation with the scriptural passage. Of course, various other methods for responding to the questions can be employed, but, in any case, it is critical to invite everyone into active participation.

5) Using application exercises:

An interactive Bible study needs to include what Walter Wink calls *application exercises*, designed to allow the participants to appropriate a key insight from the text. Assuming that participants are more deeply affected when their fuller selves are engaged (thinking, feeling, dialoguing, bodily movement, etc.), these exercises evoke more than only a left-brain response. Wink realizes that genuine transformation in our thinking and acting is disruptive and not easy. For him, this underlines the crucial value of using application exercises.

> Insights are not just fresh ideas. They are the flicker of new
> life-possibilities emerging into our sight. A moment's delay

13. See Law, *Wolf,* 113–14. See also his description of "Community Bible Study," 121–29.

in apprehending them, and the glimmer fades—they are lost. Insights are so evanescent precisely because they are foreign to the received wisdom by which we habitually operate. The transformation they promise also promises disruption of the known ways. We have a stake in receiving them; we have a stake in keeping them away. The point of the application exercises is to clear a space for insights to come; to provide the means by which they can be objectified, made tangible, visible, public; and to allow us to choose to incorporate them, with group support, into our lives.[14]

Application exercises need not be complex or take a great deal of time and can be introduced during the group's consideration of the passage. For example, invite volunteers from the group to perform physical actions described in the text. For Matt 6:1–18, have participants act out the description of the hypocrites' ostentatiously doing their pious acts. For Matt 7:1–5, invite two volunteers to perform creatively Jesus' word picture of the speck and log.

An exercise requiring more time is best reserved for concluding the group's engagement with the text. For example, have group members form pairs to dialogue about a question at the heart of the text or invite volunteers to do a role-play or share in a brief ritual action. In any case, the application exercise needs to be carefully planned and directly relevant to the insights generated by the passage itself. As Wink makes clear, every exercise used should assist the participants in making new insights *tangible* and *observable* as well as providing space for group's deep appropriation of these new life-possibilities.

Designing and facilitating application exercises is the most challenging aspect of effective leadership for interactive Bible study. Often leaders decide not to include exercises because these activities seem too risky and might meet resistance. It is important for leaders to stretch their own comfort zone in this regard and to experiment at first with simple exercises, always informing participants that they may engage in ways safe for them. Involving participants in approaching the text in an

---

14. Wink, "Engaging the Other Side of the Brain," in *Transforming*, 109. It is worth reading all of this chapter (109–27), in which Wink provides examples of what can be done strategically with biblical texts—paint pictures, write dialogues, mime, do role-play, prepare skits, work with clay, repeat holy sentences (mantras), move to music, perform physical actions, paraphrase the text, write a prayer, write a poem, read poetry, develop spontaneous rituals, use guided meditations, paint your life-line, work with two sets of texts.

experiential mode can yield rich results for the group. Predictably, deep insights that alter our vision and living come to us precisely when we are more holistically involved with a biblical passage.

6) Using music:

It is important to include music in the Bible study session because of its profound impact on people. Many traditional and newer hymns and songs are inspired by biblical texts and images. Some, especially those from the Taizé Community, are intentionally simple and use repetition to focus on memorable phrases (e.g., "Jesus, remember me when you come into your kingdom" echoing the criminal's words in Luke 23:42). For each session, I offer a selection of songs that are included in a variety of hymnals. Check the list of abbreviations to identify the full title for each hymnal abbreviation (see page xv) and the bibliography for information about the publication of each hymnal (see page 161).

Appropriate songs and music in Bible study add a powerful dimension. Singing creates in us a sharpened awareness of the reality of God's gracious reign of love and justice as well as our communal experience in Christ. Someone stated, "We sing to feel a world we can only imagine."[15] "It was Dostoevsky . . . who said that he never believed more than when he was singing the great hymns of the church."[16] Finally, to quote Carl P. Daw Jr.:

> The ideas conveyed by words that are sung root themselves in our hearts and minds much more tenaciously than those merely spoken, a phenomenon the secular world not only recognizes but even exploits through countless commercial jingles. How often the words of a hymn will return to comfort, perturb, or enlighten us, when the words of sermons, prayers, and scripture do not.[17]

15. Mary Gordon, quoting a friend who is an expert on liturgical music, in her *Circling My Mother: A Memoir*. See *The Christian Century*, 30 October 2007, 7.

16. John M. Buchanan in *The Christian Century*, 13 November 2007, 3. This issue features an article by Jeremy Begbie entitled "*Sound* Theology," 20–25.

17. These words of Dr. Carl P. Daw Jr, a hymn writer and Executive Director of The Hymn Society in the United States and Canada, were quoted in a congregational newsletter (November 2011) by Joanne Wright, then Music Director at St. Matthew Lutheran Church, Dubuque, IA.

Music gives us time to brood over the text. Music stirs our emotion. It can become a vital way to dwell in the Word and experience the power of the Spirit at work in community. For each session, it is important to include one or two songs that fit the biblical text under consideration.

7) Practicing prayerful listening:

It is important to frame the entire Bible study with prayer—in the entire group or breakout groups. Dietrich Bonhoeffer reminded us that our gathering around God's Word and Sacraments is sheer grace and should engender a thankful attitude among us.[18] It is not only appropriate but necessary to voice prayers that express that gratitude and seek help and direction from God's Spirit.

Prayer is sometimes thought to be only words we direct to God. But prayer also involves listening to God through the words of the biblical text and the responses of others in the group who reflect on the words of Jesus with their insights. Such prayerful listening is at the core of a deep engagement with Scripture.

One way to conclude the session is with a prayer circle. Invite participants to join hands in a circle and to complete first the sentence *I thank God today for . . .* and then *I ask God today for . . .* before the group prays the Lord's Prayer together. The leader will begin by sharing his or her one-sentence prayer of thanks. After sharing, the leader squeezes the hand of the person to the right. This invites the next person to share his or her prayer. If the person does not choose to share aloud, that person can simply squeeze the hand of next person. When the pulse comes back to leader after the second cycle, he or she begins the Lord's Prayer. If the group is large, participants could share either a sentence thanksgiving or petition or, if divided into subgroups, both forms of sentence prayers could be done.[19]

Prayerful experiences can be planned in various ways: free prayer whenever appropriate, a prayer planned by the leader that fits the experience, or a written prayer that all can say together. It is also appropriate to open or close the session with a song, since singing can be a form

---

18. Bonhoeffer, *Life Together,* 28.

19. Eric Law of Kaleidoscope Institute introduced this particular method for a prayer circle at a workshop I attended in Madison, WI. See the Kaleidoscope Bible Study Process described at www.kscopeinstitute.org.

of praying (e.g., a brief Taizé tune sung over and over in a meditative manner).

Bible study that makes a difference in our lives does not happen without thoughtful planning. In preparation, Bible group leaders obviously need to study and ponder seriously the text or texts under consideration. But they also need to develop ways for group participants to engage a biblical passage deeply. The methods described above—memorizing the text, asking questions, doing application exercises, pondering quotes, singing songs, and prayerful listening—can foster an atmosphere in which a group can richly "dwell in the Word." God's Spirit embraces and enhances all such efforts!

Bibliography

Bailey, Kenneth E. *Jesus Through Middle Eastern Eyes: Cultural Studies in the Gospels*. Downers Grove: InterVarsity, 2008.

Balch, David L., ed. *Social History of the Matthean Community: Cross-Disciplinary Approaches*. Minneapolis: Fortress, 1991.

Bass, Diana Butler. *Christianity for the Rest of Us: How the Neighborhood Church Is Transforming the Faith*. San Francisco: HarperSanFrancisco, 2006.

Bauer, Walter, et al. *A Greek-English Lexicon of the New Testament and Other Early Christian Literature*. 3d ed. Chicago: University of Chicago Press, 2000.

Bell, Rob. *Love Wins: A Book About Heaven, Hell, and the Fate of Every Person Who Ever Lived*. New York: HarperOne, 2011.

Betz, Hans Dieter. *Essays on the Sermon on the Mount*. Translated by L. L. Welborn. Philadelphia: Fortress, 1985.

—————. *The Sermon on the Mount: A Commentary on the Sermon on the Mount, including the Sermon on the Plain (Matthew 5:3—7:27 and Luke 6:20-49)*. Hermeneia. Minneapolis: Fortress, 1995.

Bok, Sissela. *Lying: Moral Choice in Public and Private Life*. New York: Pantheon, 1978.

Boomershine, Thomas E. *Story Journey: An Invitation to the Gospel as Storytelling*. Nashville: Abingdon, 1988.

Bonhoeffer, Dietrich. *Discipleship*. Edited by Geffrey B. Kelly and John D. Godsey and translated by Barbara Green and Reinhard Krauss. Minneapolis: Fortress, 2001.

—————. *Life Together* and *Prayerbook of the Bible*. Edited by Geffrey B. Kelly and translated by Daniel W. Bloesch and James H. Burtness. Minneapolis: Fortress, 1996.

Bosch, David J. *Transforming Mission: Paradigm Shifts in Theology of Mission*. Maryknoll, NY: Orbis, 1991.

Brueggemann, Walter. *The Prophetic Imagination*. Minneapolis: Fortress, 1978.

Buber, Martin. "Teaching and Deed" (Address delivered at the Lehrhaus in Frankfort on the Main in 1934). In *Israel and the World: Essays in a Time of Crisis*, 137–45. 1948. Reprint, New York: Schocken, 1963.

Clements, Ronald E. *In Spirit and in Truth: Insights from Biblical Prayers*. Atlanta: John Knox, 1985.

Copenhaver, Martin B. "Decide or Discern." *Christian Century* 127:26 (28 December 2010).

Covey, Stephen R., et al. *First Things First: To Live, to Love, to Learn, to Leave a Legacy*. New York: Free Press, 1993.

Bibliography

Crosby, Michael H. *Spirituality of the Beatitudes: Matthew's Challenge for First World Christians.* Maryknoll, NY: Orbis, 1980.

The Dead Sea Scrolls: A New Translation. Translated by Michael Wise et al. San Francisco: Harper Collins, 1996.

Deci, Edward L. "Effects of Externally Mediated Rewards on Intrinsic Motivation." *Journal of Personality and Social Psychology* 18:1 (1971) 105–115.

The Didache. In *The Apostolic Fathers,* vol. 1 of the Loeb Classical Library. Cambridge: Harvard University Press, 1912.

Donders, Joseph G. *Jesus, Heaven on Earth: Reflections on the Gospels for the A-Cycle.* Maryknoll, NY: Orbis, 1980.

Dunn, James D. G. *Jesus Remembered.* Vol. 1 of *Christianity in the Making.* Grand Rapids: Eerdmans, 2003.

Ellsberg, Robert, ed. *By Little and By Little: The Selected Writings of Dorothy Day.* New York: Knopf, 1983.

Evangelical Lutheran Church in America. *Evangelical Lutheran Worship.* Minneapolis: Augsburg Fortress, 2006.

Fabrick, Stephen Dillon. *Us & Them: Moderating Group Conflict.* 2004. Online: http://www.psysr.org.

The Faith We Sing. Nashville: Abingdon, 2000.

Fendall, Lon, et al. *Practicing Discernment Together: Finding God's Way Forward in Decision Making.* Newberg, OR: Barclay, 2007.

Fleer, David, and Dave Bland, eds. *Preaching the Sermon on the Mount: The World It Imagines.* St. Louis: Chalice, 2007.

Freedman, David Noel, ed. *The Anchor Bible Dictionary.* 6 vols. New York: Doubleday, 1992.

Fortune, Marie M. Faith Trust Institute. Online: http://www.faithtrustinstitute.org.

Gilkey, Langdon. *Shantung Compound: The Story of Men and Women Under Pressure.* New York: Harper & Row, 1966.

Glory to God: The Presbyterian Hymnal. Presbyterian Publishing Incorporation, 2013.

Hallie, Philip P. *Lest Innocent Blood Be Shed.* New York: HarperPerennial, 1979 (with Introduction, 1994).

Hanson, K. C., and Douglas E. Oakman. *Palestine in the Time of Jesus: Social Structures and Social Conflicts.* 2d ed. Minneapolis: Fortress, 2008.

Hauerwas, Stanley, and William H. Willimon. *Resident Aliens.* Nashville: Abingdon, 1989.

Hearon, Holly E., and Philip Ruge-Jones, eds. *The Bible in Ancient and Modern Media: Story and Performance.* Eugene, OR: Cascade, 2009.

Horsley, Richard A. *Jesus and the Spiral of Violence: Popular Jewish Resistance in Roman Palestine.* San Francisco: Harper & Row, 1987.

The Hymnal 1982, according to the use of The Episcopal Church. New York: Church Publishing Incorporated, 1985.

Hymns for the Gospels. Chicago: GIA, 2001.

Isenhower, Valerie K., and Judith A. Todd. *Listen for God's Leading: A Workbook for Corporate Spiritual Discernment.* Nashville: Upper Room, 2009.

Jankowski, Martin. *Der Tag, der Deutschland Veränderte.* Leipzig: Evangelische Verlagsanstalt, 2007.

Jeremias, Joachim. *The Lord's Prayer.* Translated by John Reumann. Philadelphia: Fortress, Facet, 1964.

————. *The Prayers of Jesus.* Translated by John Bowden et al. Philadelphia: Fortress, 1967.

Jordan, Clarence. *Sermon on the Mount.* Rev. ed. Valley Forge: Judson, 1952.

Keen, Sam. *Faces of the Enemy: Reflections on the Hostile Imagination.* San Francisco: Harper & Row, 1986.

Keifert, Patrick. *We Are Here Now: A New Missional Era.* Eagle, ID: Allelon, 2006.

Kolb, Robert, and Timothy J. Wengert, eds. *The Book of Concord: The Confessions of the Evangelical Lutheran Church.* Minneapolis: Fortress, 2000.

Law, Eric H. F. *The Wolf Shall Dwell with the Lamb: A Spirituality for Leadership in a Multicultural Community.* St. Louis: Chalice, 1993.

Lee, Margaret Ellen, and Bernard Brandon Scott. *Sound Mapping the New Testament.* Salem, OR: Polebridge, 2009.

Lutheran Book of Worship. Prepared by Lutheran Church in America, The American Lutheran Church, The Evangelical Lutheran Church of Canada, and The Lutheran Church—Missouri Synod. Minneapolis: Augsburg, 1978.

Luz, Ulrich. *Matthew 1–7: A Commentary.* Translated by Wilhelm C. Linss. Minneapolis: Augsburg, 1989.

MacMullen, Ramsay. *Roman Social Relations: 50 B.C. to A.D. 284.* New Haven: Yale University Press, 1974.

Malina Bruce J., and Richard L. Rohrbaugh. *Social-Science Commentary on the Synoptic Gospels.* 2d ed. Minneapolis: Fortress, 2003.

Milgrom, Jacob. *Leviticus 1–16.* The Anchor Bible. New York: Doubleday, 1991.

————. *Leviticus 17–22.* The Anchor Bible. New York: Doubleday, 2000.

The Mishnah. Translated by Jacob Neusner. New Haven: Yale University Press, 1988.

Morris, G. H. "Finding Fault." *Journal of Language and Social Psychology* 7:1 (1988). Online: http://jls.sagepub.com/content/7/1/1.full.pdf.

Murphy-O'Connor, Jerome. *The Holy Land: An Archaeological Guide from Earliest Times to 1700.* 2d ed. Oxford & New York: Oxford University Press, 1986.

Nessan, Craig L. *Give Us This Day: A Lutheran Proposal for Ending World Hunger.* Minneapolis: Augsburg Fortress, 2003.

The New Century Hymnal. Cleveland: Pilgrim, 1995.

New Revised Standard Version Bible. New York: Division of Christian Education of the National Council of the Churches of Christ in the United States of America, 1989.

Nouwen, Henri J. M. *Life of the Beloved: Spiritual Living in a Secular World.* Tenth anniversary ed. New York: Crossroad, 1992.

Novogratz, Jacqueline. *The Blue Sweater: Bridging the Gap between Rich and Poor in an Interconnected World.* New York: Roldale, 2009.

Oden, Thomas C. *Structure of Awareness.* Nashville: Abingdon, 1969.

The Presbyterian Hymnal: Hymns, Psalms, and Spiritual Songs. Louisville: Westminster / John Knox, 1990.

Rhoads, David. "What Is Performance Criticism?" In *The Bible in Ancient and Modern Media: Story and Performance*, edited by Holly E. Hearon and Philip Ruge-Jones. Eugene, OR: Cascade, 2009.

Roxburgh, Alan J., and Fred Romanuk. *The Missional Leader: Equipping Your Church to Reach a Changing World.* San Francisco: Jossey-Bass, 2006.

Sing the Faith. Louisville: Geneva, 2003.

Stark, Rodney. "Antioch as the Social Situation for Matthew's Gospel." In *Social History of the Matthean Community: Cross-Disciplinary Approaches*, edited by David L. Balch, 189–210. Minneapolis: Fortress, 1991.

Stegemann, Ekkehard W., and Wolfgang Stegemann. *The Jesus Movement: A Social History of Its First Century*. Translated by O. C. Dean Jr. Minneapolis: Fortress, 1999.

Suchocki, Marjorie Hewitt. *In God's Presence: Theological Reflections on Prayer*. St. Louis: Chalice, 1996.

Talbert, Charles H. *Reading the Sermon on the Mount: Character Formation and Decision Making in Matthew 5–7*. Grand Rapids: Baker Academic, 2004.

Tavris, Carol. *Anger: The Misunderstood Emotion*. Rev. ed. New York: Simon & Schuster, 1989.

Tavris, Carol, and Elliot Aronson. *Mistakes Were Made (But Not by Me): Why We Justify Foolish Beliefs, Bad Decisions, and Hurtful Acts*. New York: Harcourt, 2007.

Taylor, Barbara Brown. *When God is Silent*. The 1997 Lyman Beecher Lectures on Preaching. Cambridge, MA: Cowley, 1998.

Taylor, Shelly E. *Positive Illusions: Creative Self-Deception and the Healthy Mind*. New York: Basic Books, 1989.

This Far by Faith: An African American Resource for Worship. Minneapolis: Augsburg Fortress, 1999.

The United Methodist Hymnal: Book of United Methodist Worship. Nashville: United Methodist Publishing, 1989.

Via, Dan O. Jr. *Self-Deception and Wholeness in Paul and Matthew*. Minneapolis: Fortress, 1990.

Westhelle, Vítor. *The Scandalous God: The Use and Abuse of the Cross*. Minneapolis: Fortress, 2006.

Wilken, Robert L. *The Land Called Holy: Palestine in Christian History and Thought*. New Haven and London: Yale University Press, 1992.

Wink, Walter. *Engaging the Powers: Discernment and Resistance in a World of Domination*. Minneapolis: Fortress, 1992.

———. *Transforming Bible Study: A Leader's Guide*. Nashville: Abingdon, 1980.

With One Voice: A Lutheran Resource for Worship. Minneapolis: Augsburg Fortress, 1995.

Worship & Praise: Songbook. Minneapolis: Augsburg Fortress, 1999.

Worship & Rejoice. Carol Stream, IL: Hope Publishing, 2001.

Worship & Song. Nashville: Abingdon, 2011.

Wright, N. T. *The Lord and His Prayer*. Grand Rapids: Eerdmans, 1996.

Ylvisaker, John. *Borning Cry: Hymns, Anthems and Biblical Songs*. 2 vols. 2d ed. Waverly, IA: New Generation, 2002.

Ancient Document Index

Mark

Made in the USA
Lexington, KY
27 February 2014